Best Easy Day Hikes Series

Best Easy Day Hikes
San Antonio

Keith Stelter

FALCONGUIDES

GUILFORD, CONNECTICUT
HELENA, MONTANA

AN IMPRINT OF GLOBE PEQUOT PRESS

FALCONGUIDES®

Project editor: Jessica Haberman
Layout: Kevin Mak
Maps: Off Route Inc. © Morris Book Publishing, LLC

TOPO! Explorer software and SuperQuad source maps courtesy of National Geographic Maps. For information about TOPO! Explorer, TOPO!, and Nat Geo Maps products, go to www.topo.com or www .natgeomaps.com.

Library of Congress Cataloging-in-Publication Data is available on file.

ISBN 978-0-7627-5297-3

Printed in the United States of America
10 9 8 7 6 5 4 3 2 1

Contents

San Antonio Overview

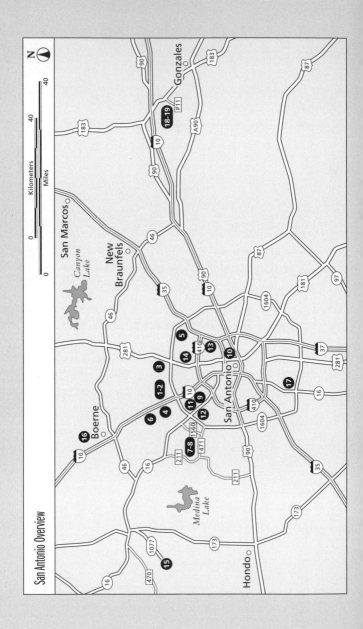

Acknowledgments

Many people helped make this book possible, and a few went "beyond the call of duty." Thanks to Mark, Scott, and Kay Stelter for their encouragement, ideas, and proofreading. Nicole and Jessica Stelter helped with filing and sorting papers. Karen Vasquez and Rick and Samantha Finch went hiking with me.

Thanks also to Chris Holmes, Texas Parks & Wildlife Department (TPWD) regional interpretive specialist, State Parks Region V, for working with me on new trails and the development of Texas Parks & Wildlife trail maps. There were many other folks at TPWD who were very helpful. Thanks to Dianne Hart, GIS specialist for San Antonio Natural Areas, who helped with making trail maps.

There were dozens of other people who helped with information about history, geology, flora and fauna, and hikes they considered "the best." I appreciate their work and thank all of them.

Introduction

The purpose of this book is to offer more than the typical hiking guide, in which most trail descriptions are generally point-to-point guides, getting you from the trailhead to the trail's end. This book provides details about flora, fauna, history, and geology to appeal to a broad spectrum of hikers, including families with young children. I spent nine months researching, talking with rangers and other folks, hiking, and sometimes rehiking a trail, studying the area and looking for interesting facts, scenery, history, geology, and topography. I talked with a variety of hikers, asking them what they wanted a hike to cover and what made a "best hike." I had the best overall hiking region in Texas to choose from—central Texas, which includes the Edwards Plateau and the Hill Country.

I used the following criteria to come up with the best hikes included in this guide: accessibility, fun, exercise, family experience, scenery, history, rivers and lakes, experience of the hiker, moderate length (approximately 2 to 4 miles), dog friendliness, and wheelchair accessibility. Loops and preferably interconnecting loop trails were selected where possible, so a "best" hike within a park could be fashioned by combining the best of several trails.

Determining the "best" hikes in the area was a combination of personal judgment about who the hike would appeal to and information from park staff and other hikers. Four of my favorite hikes are in the following parks: Friedrich Wilderness Park, Palmetto State Park, Comanche Lookout, and Government Canyon State Natural Area.

Trails are no longer the exclusive domain of the solitude-loving wilderness seeker or the dedicated fitness enthusiast. Whether providing recreational and educational opportunities, encouraging well-being, exploring history and geology, or bringing together people of all ages, hiking has become an important factor in many people's lives. I hope that at least some of these hikes will become your best hikes and that the book will be informative and interesting reading, as well as an excellent guide.

San Antonio Weather

The San Antonio climate is subtropical, with an average low temperature in January of 39°F and an average high in July and August of 95°F. The average yearly rainfall is 30 inches. The wettest month is May, averaging 4.2 inches. The driest month is March with 1.6 inches of rain, followed closely by January and December with 1.7 inches. The city generally has mild temperatures with 300 days of sunshine a year.

State Parks Pass

For the best deal around, take advantage of the Texas State Parks Pass instead of paying on a per-person/per-visit basis. The pass provides entry to all ninety-three state parks for the member and all occupants of his or her vehicle. It's good for one year from time of purchase. Purchase at the park or order by phone: (512) 389-8900.

Flora and Fauna

The hiking trails around San Antonio, including portions of the Texas Hill Country, have a biodiversity hard to equal. The merging of four major ecoregions—the post oak savanna, the blackland prairie, the south Texas plains, and the Edwards Plateau—is part of the reason. Another is that the Central Flyway, one of four major bird migration routes in the United States, goes directly over the area. More than 400 of the 600 bird species recorded in the state have been seen in this region. The golden-cheeked warbler and black-capped vireo, both endangered species, are native to Texas. The golden-cheeked warbler nests only in central Texas. Several of the hikes, particularly at Balcones Canyonlands National Wildlife Refuge, offer good viewing.

The best indication of birds being present is hearing their songs. The Carolina chickadee sings "chickadee-dee-dee-dee," the killdeer "kildee, kildee, kildee," and woodpeckers "rat-atap-rat." The northern mockingbird, the Texas state bird, can be heard mimicking the calls of other birds. Texans claim the mockingbird has the prettiest song of any bird. Some of the most colorful birds include the black-crested tit-mouse, ladder-backed woodpecker, painted bunting, road-runner, northern cardinal, eastern bluebird, red-shouldered hawk, great blue heron, and numerous ducks. Millions of Mexican free-tailed bats, the state flying mammal, arrive in central Texas each spring to roost in caves in the Balcones Escarpment and the Edwards Plateau.

Most mammals are active during the night, so seeing them can be difficult. Look for their tracks around the trail and near streams or lakes. White-tailed deer, nine-banded armadillos (the state small mammal), coyote, bobcat, beaver, opossum, ring-tailed cat, badger, fox, raccoon, skunk, wild hogs, javelina, fox squirrels, and Rio Grande wild turkeys make their homes here. White-tailed deer are abundant in many of the hiking areas.

Some trees and plants native to east Texas seem to be constantly meeting those of west Texas in transitional zones or isolated pockets. The dwarf palmettos in Palmetto State Park are an example. Rivers and creeks are lined with bald cypress, black willow, hackberry, sycamore, cottonwood, and pecan. Bald cypress trees add a majestic dimension to waterways, towering up to 120 feet with their cone-shaped "knees" projecting up through the water. Pecan trees, the state tree, also like river shores.

The upland areas contain a mix of deciduous and evergreen trees, including Ashe's juniper, live oak, red oak, bigtooth maple, and Texas persimmon. The live oak is an unusual species because it is an evergreen oak tree. Spanish moss can be seen hanging from oaks, bald cypress, and other trees. The Ashe's juniper not only furnishes nesting material for the endangered golden-cheeked warbler, but its berries also provide food for berry-foraging wildlife. The Ashe's juniper's blue-black seed cones, known as juniper berries, are used to flavor gin.

In spring and early summer, when wildflowers set the roadsides ablaze with color, driving to a hiking location can be a visual feast. Commonly seen are coreopsis (yellow), firewheels (red), phlox, Mexican hats, daisies, winecups (purple), yellow primrose, bluestem grass, and prickly pear cactus. The cactus has spectacular red and yellow blooms from early spring to summer. The Texas bluebonnet, the state flower, is at its peak in late March and early April.

The diversity of wildflowers attracts many butterfly species. The monarch, the state insect, is unique among butterflies because of its extremely long migration flight. During the spring and the fall migration, millions of monarchs pass through the area. The Balcones Canyonlands

National Wildlife Refuge is an excellent location to see the butterflies.

The great ecological diversity of the territory, along with the flora and fauna, allow trips to be fashioned that are much more than just a "hike in the woods."

Enjoy the experience of hiking central Texas.

Wildlife and Bird Viewing Trails

The Texas Parks & Wildlife Department has developed two sets of maps showing prime viewing locations for wildlife and birds. The Heart of Texas Wildlife Trails has an eastern section identified as HOTE and a western section identified as HOTW. The Great Texas Coastal Birding Trail–Central Coast was developed to showcase premier birding sites. These are identified with a CTC, and there are ninety-five unique sites.

Texas was the first state in the nation to create birding and wildlife viewing trails. Some of these sites have viewing blinds. If the possibility of hearing or seeing an endangered species exists, a note identifies the species under the park location. Golden-cheeked warblers nest only in central Texas. Using these maps can give an added dimension to hiking, including great photo opportunities. More information about these trails and maps, including where to purchase them, can be found at the TPWD Web site: www.tpwd.state.tx.us.

Zero Impact and Trail Etiquette

We have a responsibility to protect, no longer just conquer and use, our wild places. Many public hiking locations are at risk, so please do what you can to use them wisely. The following section will help you understand better what it means to take care of parks and wild places while still making the most of your hiking experience. Anyone can take a hike, but hiking safely and with good conservation practices is an art requiring preparation and proper equipment. Always leave an area as good as—or preferably better than—you found it.

- **Stay on the trail.** It's true—a path anywhere leads nowhere new, but purists will just have to get over it. Paths serve an important purpose: They limit impact on natural areas. Straying from a designated trail may seem innocent but it can cause damage to sensitive areas— damage that may take years to recover from, if they can recover at all. Even simple shortcuts can be destructive. Many of the hikes described in this guide are on or near areas ecologically important to supporting endangered flora and fauna. So, please, stay on the trail.

- **Leave no weeds.** Noxious weeds tend to overtake other plants, which in turn affects animals and birds that depend on them for food. To minimize the spread of noxious weeds, hikers should regularly clean their boots and hiking poles of mud and seeds. Nonnative invasive plants are particularly destructive and can quickly destroy acres of habitat. Yaupon is an example. Brush your dog to remove any weed seeds before heading off into a new area. Keep your dog under control. Always obey leash laws, and be sure to bury your dog's waste or pack it in resealable plastic bags.

- **Respect other trail users.** Often you're not the only one on the trail. With the rise in popularity of multiuse trails, you'll have to learn a new kind of respect, beyond the nod and "hello" approach of the past. First investigate whether you're on a multiuse trail, and assume the appropriate precautions. If you hear activity ahead, step off the trail just to be safe.

Mountain bikers can be like stealth airplanes—you may not hear them coming. Be prepared and find out ahead of time whether you share the trail with them. Cyclists should always yield to hikers, but that's little comfort to the hiker. Be aware.

When you approach horses or pack animals on the trail, always step quietly off the trail, preferably on the downhill side, and let them pass.

More trails are being designed to be, at least in part, wheelchair accessible. Always step to the side to allow folks in wheelchairs time to navigate the terrain. Make them aware if you are going to pass around them.

First Aid

Sunburn

Take along sunscreen or sunblock, protective clothing, and a wide-brimmed hat. If you do get a sunburn, protect the area from further sun exposure and treat the area with a remedy of your choice. Remember that your eyes are vulnerable to damaging radiation as well.

Blisters

Be prepared to take care of these hike-spoilers by carrying moleskin (a lightly padded adhesive), gauze, and tape. An effective way to apply moleskin is to cut out a circle of moleskin, remove the center—like a doughnut—and place it over the blistered area. Cutting the center out will reduce the pressure applied to the sensitive skin.

Insect Bites and Stings

You can treat most insect bites and stings by applying hydro-cortisone cream (1 percent solution) topically. Remove any stingers by using tweezers or scraping the area with your fingernail or a knife blade. Don't pinch the area, as you'll only spread the venom. Some hikers are highly sensitive to bites and stings and may have a serious allergic reaction that can be life threatening. Symptoms of a serious allergic reaction can include wheezing, an asthmatic attack, and shock.

Ticks

Ticks can carry diseases such as Rocky Mountain spotted fever and Lyme disease. The best defense is, of course, prevention. If you know you're going to be hiking through an area containing ticks, wear long pants and a long-sleeved shirt. You can apply a permethrin repellent to your clothing and a DEET repellent to exposed skin. At the end of your hike, do a spot check for ticks (and insects in general). If you do find a tick, coat the insect with petroleum jelly or tree sap to cut off its air supply. The tick should release its hold, but if it doesn't, grab the head of the tick firmly—with a pair of tweezers if you have them—and gently pull it away from the skin with a twisting motion. Clean the affected area with an antibacterial cleanser and then apply triple-antibiotic ointment. Monitor the area for a few days. If irritation persists or a white spot develops, see a doctor for possible infection.

Poison Ivy, Oak, and Sumac

These skin irritants are prevalent on many of the trails in central Texas, sometimes growing into the trail. They come in the form of a bush or a vine, having leaflets in groups of three (poison ivy and oak), five, seven, or nine. Learn how to spot the plants, and especially show young children what to look for. Few things can spoil a hike, or your life the week after, more than accidentally getting poison ivy. The oil secreted by the plant can cause an allergic reaction in the form of blisters, usually about twelve hours after exposure. The itchy rash can last from ten days to several weeks.

The best defense against these irritants is to wear clothing that covers the arms, legs, and torso. For summer, zip-off cargo pants come in handy. There are also nonprescription lotions you can apply to exposed skin that guard against the effects of poison ivy, oak, or sumac and can be washed off with soap and water. If you think you were in contact with the plants, after hiking (or even on the trail during longer hikes) wash with soap and water. If the rash spreads, either tough it out or see your doctor.

Natural Hazards

Besides tripping over a rock or tree root on the trail, there are some real hazards to be aware of while hiking, including a few weather conditions you may need to take into account.

Lightning
Thunderstorms build over some areas in central Texas almost every day during the summer. Lightning is generated by thunderheads and can strike without warning, even several miles away from the nearest cloud. The best rule of thumb is to start leaving exposed peaks, ridges, and canyon rims by about noon if the weather forecast includes thunderstorms. This time can vary a little depending on storm buildup. Keep an eye on cloud formation, and don't underestimate how fast a storm can build. Lightning takes the

path of least resistance, so if you're the high point, it might choose you. Ducking under a rock overhang is dangerous as you form the shortest path between the rock and ground. Avoid having both your hands and feet touching the ground at once and never lie flat. If you hear a buzzing sound or feel your hair standing on end, move quickly, as an electrical charge is building up.

The National Weather Service provides these cautions:

- If you can hear thunder, you are in striking distance of lightning.
- Suspend outdoor activities during thunderstorms and lightning.
- Get off high ground.
- Do not stay under trees.
- Get into an enclosed building or enclosed vehicle.

Flash Floods

In July 2007 a torrential downpour (17 inches in twenty-four hours) dumped tons of water into the Marble Falls area near several state parks and hiking trails. Flash flooding, a phenomenon of the Hill Country, flooded trails, homes, and cities and washed away sections of highways. The spooky thing about flash floods, especially in Hill Country canyons and streambeds, is that they can appear out of nowhere, generated by a storm many miles away. While hiking or driving in canyons, keep an eye on the weather. Always climb to safety if danger threatens. Flash floods usually subside quickly, so be patient and don't cross a swollen stream.

Now prepare for your next hike, remembering our responsibilities as modern-day hikers to do our part in conserving the outdoors. Enjoy.

How to Use This Guide

Nineteen hikes are detailed in this book. To aid in quick decision-making, each hike description begins with a hike summary. These short summaries give you a taste of the hiking adventure to follow. You'll learn about the trail terrain and what surprises the route has to offer.

Each hike is accompanied by a route map that shows accessible roads and trails, points of interest, access to water, towns, landmarks, and geographical features. It also distinguishes trails from roads, and paved roads from unpaved roads. The selected route is highlighted, and directional arrows point the way.

Next you'll find the quick, nitty-gritty details of the hike: where the trailhead is located, hike length, approximate hiking time, difficulty rating, type of trail surface, other trail users, canine compatibility, land status, fees and permits, trail hours, map resources, trail contacts, and other information that will help you on your trek.

Finding the trailhead provides directions from a nearby city or town right down to where you'll want to park your car.

The Hike is the meat of the chapter. Detailed and honest, it's a carefully researched impression of the trail. While it's impossible to cover everything, you can rest assured that you won't miss what's important.

Miles and Directions provides mileage cues that identify all turns and trail name changes, as well as points of interest.

Don't feel restricted to the routes and trails mapped in this guide. Be adventurous and use the book as a platform to discover new routes for yourself, but do stick to designated trails. One of the simplest ways to begin is to turn the map upside down and hike the trail in reverse. The change in perspective can make the hike feel quite different; it's like getting two hikes for one.

You may wish to copy the directions for the course onto a small sheet to help you while hiking, or photocopy the map and Miles and Directions to take with you. Otherwise, just slip the whole book in your backpack and take it with you. Enjoy your time in the outdoors, and remember to pack out what you pack in.

Map Legend

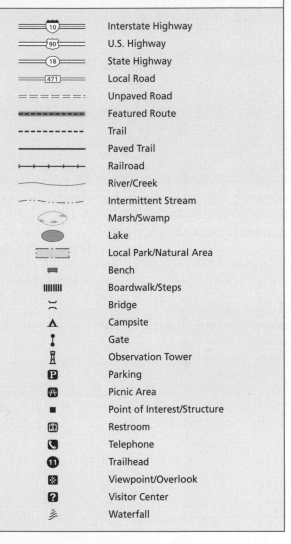	Interstate Highway
	U.S. Highway
	State Highway
	Local Road
	Unpaved Road
	Featured Route
	Trail
	Paved Trail
	Railroad
	River/Creek
	Intermittent Stream
	Marsh/Swamp
	Lake
	Local Park/Natural Area
	Bench
	Boardwalk/Steps
	Bridge
	Campsite
	Gate
	Observation Tower
	Parking
	Picnic Area
	Point of Interest/Structure
	Restroom
	Telephone
	Trailhead
	Viewpoint/Overlook
	Visitor Center
	Waterfall

1 Eisenhower Park: Hillview, Red Oak, and Cedar Flats Trails

The Hillview and Cedar Flats Trails have been combined into a counterclockwise loop. This provides a range of hiking from easy to moderate through some of the most scenic sections of the 320-acre park. Cedar Flats Trail is wheelchair and stroller accessible.

Distance: 3.1-mile loop
Approximate hiking time: 2.5 hours
Difficulty: Moderate due to some limestone outcrops on Hillview Trail
Trail surface: Hillview is crushed gravel and rock. Cedar Flats is asphalt.
Best seasons: Year-round
Other trail users: Dog walkers, joggers
Canine compatibility: Leashed dogs permitted
Land status: San Antonio natural area park; San Antonio Parks and Recreation Department

Fees and permits: None required
Schedule: 6:00 a.m. to sunset daily; closed Christmas and New Year's Day
Maps: Available at www.san naturalareas.org; USGS Castle Hills
Trail contacts: Friedrich Wilderness Park, 21395 Milsa Rd., San Antonio 78256; (210) 564-6400. NOTE: Friedrich is headquarters for natural areas.
Special considerations: No in-line skates, scooters, or bicycles are allowed. Restrooms and water are at the trailhead.

Finding the trailhead: From downtown, take I-10 west to Loop 1604 East (Anderson Loop). Stay on Loop 1604 for 1.5 miles, then take the exit for FM 1535, Shavano Park & Military Highway. Turn left onto Northwest Military Highway and follow it for 1.6 miles. The park entrance is at 19399 Northwest Military Hwy. on the left. Eisenhower

Park is about 19 miles northwest of downtown. *DeLorme: Texas Atlas & Gazetteer:* Page 156 A3. GPS: N 29 37.295' / W 98 34.466'

The Hike

This Hillview Trail starts near the kiosk, which features a large trail map and pocket-size maps. Be sure to take one of the small maps that also include an interpretive guide for plants that are identified by short marker posts along the trail. The guide was an Eagle Scout project of Boy Scout Troop 650. Restroom facilities and water fountains are available. Parts of these trails have no shade, so wear a hat and sunscreen, and take plenty of water.

Head north, passing by the intersection with Yucca Trail. The surface on the first 0.25 mile is asphalt; it then changes to crushed gravel and limestone. Hillview Trail contains some of the most rugged sections of the hike as it leads to Red Oak Trail. There are a number of Y branches, so follow the Miles and Directions instructions.

Continue heading north, and then make a sharp bend left, heading west along the park boundary. Pass by groups of prickly pear cactus, the state plant. The trail undulates up and down but generally heads up. Cedar trees form a partial canopy. Go by the first junction on the left (south) with Shady Creek Trail, and within 100 yards pass the second junction. Continue following Hillview west.

The surface becomes increasingly rougher as it heads up over limestone outcrops, jokingly called "steps," and across tree roots. This is the most difficult part of the hike; fortunately, some of the rocks have flat surfaces that can be used to sit on. Watch for numbered, low interpretive marker posts. Pass an intersection on the left with Yucca Trail. Continue following Hillview to a Y intersection with Red

Eisenhower Park: Hillview, Red Oak, and Cedar Flats Trails

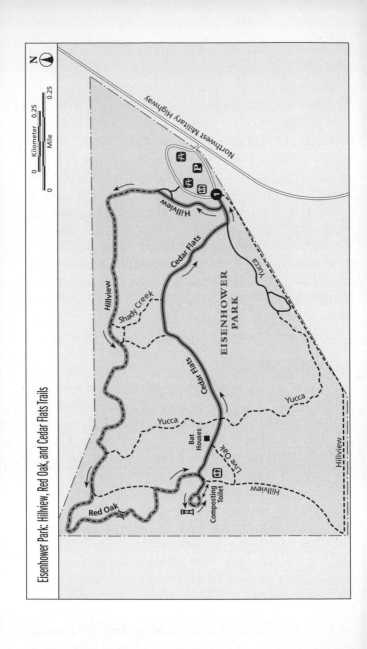

Oak. Take the right branch onto Red Oak, heading west and then north for a short distance.

Follow Red Oak as it bends sharply left, heading south along the park's western boundary. This is a less traveled part and one of the best areas to see wildlife. Cross a wooden bridge over a dry creek bed, continuing south, and then make a hard right (east) to reach the T with Hillview. Take the right branch, heading a short distance south, where it Y's into Cedar Flats.

Follow Cedar Flats west, past a composting toilet and to the observation tower. There are some good views over the trees, but they are marred by a quarry and some power lines in the direction toward San Antonio. Backtrack and follow Cedar Flats Trail east. Pass by two tall poles on the left that support bat houses. Continue past two intersections on the left with Shady Creek Trail and head southeast to the trailhead.

Miles and Directions

0.0 Start at the Hillview Trail trailhead.

0.1 Pass Yucca Trail on the left. Continue on Hillview.

0.2 Reach a Y and take the left branch heading north by north-east. Within 200 feet reach another Y and take the left branch heading north.

0.7 Reach a junction with Shady Creek Trail on the left (south). Continue straight (north) on Hillview. The remaining mile of this trail has some challenging sections with limestone outcrops and tree roots across it.

1.0 The top of the ridge has been reached, but panoramic views are blocked by trees. Follow Hillview, heading slightly down.

1.2 Reach a Y and take the right branch, continuing straight on Hillview. The left branch is Yucca Trail.

1.4 Reach a Y and take the right branch heading east on Red Oak Trail. Follow Red Oak as it heads west and then south.

1.7 Cross a 25-foot-long wooden bridge over a dry creek bed. Continue following Red Oak south and then bear left (west).

1.9 Reach a T where Red Oak ends at Hillview. Take the right branch on Hillview, heading south.

2.1 Reach a T with Cedar Flats Trail. Take the right branch heading southwest. Cedar Flats is an asphalt trail. Almost immediately reach a composting toilet. Follow Cedar Flats right when it Y's with Hillview. Go about 100 yards northwest and reach the observation tower. Then backtrack to the Y where Cedar Flats and Hillview join.

2.2 Take the right branch at the Y with Hillview and Cedar Flats, heading east and then bearing northeast.

2.4 Yucca Trail crosses Cedar Flats. Continue following Cedar Flats east.

2.5 Reach a Y and take the right branch, continuing east on Cedar Flats. The left branch is Shady Creek Trail.

2.6 Pass the west leg of Shady Creek Trail as it dead-ends into Cedar Flats. Continue following Cedar Flats east and then bear southeast.

2.9 Reach a T and take the left branch, heading east on Yucca Trail. Follow Yucca Trail back to the trailhead.

3.1 Arrive back at the trailhead.

2 Eisenhower Park: Yucca, Shady Creek, and Cedar Flats Trails

Eisenhower Park, with its 320 acres and over 5 miles of trails, allows hikers to choose from paved, relatively flat trails or rocky, natural–surface, strenuous hikes. This hike offers some of both. Cedar Flats Trail and sections of Yucca Trail are wheelchair and stroller accessible.

Distance: 1.9-mile clockwise loop

Approximate hiking time: 1 hour

Difficulty: Easy except for 0.3-mile Shady Creek Trail, which is moderate

Trail surface: Asphalt except for Shady Creek Trail's stone and limestone outcrops.

Best seasons: Year-round

Other trail users: Dog walkers, joggers

Canine compatibility: Leashed dogs permitted

Land status: San Antonio natural area park; San Antonio Parks and Recreation Department

Fees and permits: None required

Schedule: 6:00 a.m. to sunset daily; closed Christmas and New Year's Day

Maps: Available at www.sannaturalareas.org; USGS Castle Hills

Trail contacts: Friedrich Wilderness Park, 21395 Milsa Rd., San Antonio 78256; (210) 564-6400. Note: Friedrich is headquarters for natural areas.

Special considerations: No in-line skates, scooters, or bicycles are allowed. Restrooms and water are at the trailhead.

Finding the trailhead: From downtown, take I-10 west to Loop 1604 East (Anderson Loop). Stay on Loop 1604 for 1.5 miles, then take the exit for FM 1535, Shavano Park & Military Highway. Turn left onto Northwest Military Highway and follow it for 1.6 miles. The park entrance is at 19399 Northwest Military Hwy. on the left. Eisenhower

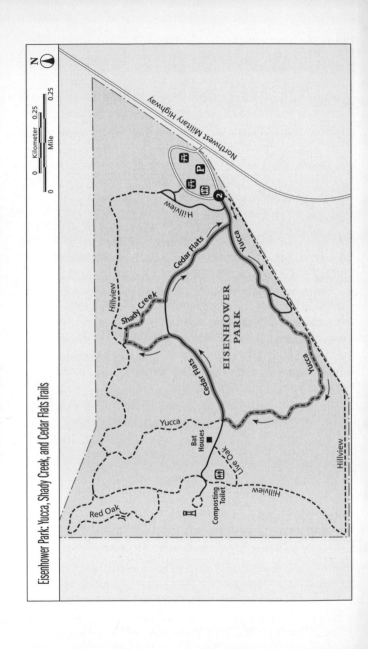

Eisenhower Park: Yucca, Shady Creek, and Cedar Flats Trails

N

0   Kilometer   0.25

0   Mile   0.25

Northwest Military Highway

Hillview

Cedar Flats

Shady Creek

Yucca

Hillview

EISENHOWER PARK

Cedar Flats

Yucca

Yucca

Hillview

Bat Houses

Live Oak

Composting Toilet

Red Oak

Park is about 19 miles northwest of downtown. *DeLorme: Texas Atlas & Gazetteer:* Page 156 A3. GPS: N 29 37.295' / W 98 34.466'

The Hike

The combined Yucca/Cedar Flats/Shady Creek Trail hike starts near the kiosk, which features a large trail map and pocket-size maps. Be sure to take one of the small maps that also include an interpretive guide for plants that are identified by short marker posts along the trail. The guide was an Eagle Scout project of Boy Scout Troop 650. Restroom facilities and water fountains are available. Parts of these trails have no shade, so wear a hat and sunscreen, and take plenty of water.

Head southwest from the Yucca trailhead and follow the paved trail along the southwest park boundary. In a short distance pass the intersection, on the right, with Cedar Flats Trail. Pass by some prickly pear cactus. In spring they can have spectacular yellow and red blooms. Even though cedars and small live oaks border the trail, there is little shade. There are benches at intervals alongside the trail.

In about 0.25 mile reach a Y that leads to a small loop in the Yucca Trail. Take the right branch, continuing southwest. The trail surface changes to shredded cedar. The trail squiggles right and left as it approaches a hard right bend, heading north. In the spring and fall, watch for a variety of butterflies. Portions of the trail have an arching cover of cedars, providing welcome shade.

About 1 mile from the trailhead, reach the T junction with the asphalt-paved Cedar Flats Trail. Take the right branch, heading east by northeast toward the junction with Shady Creek. The trail slopes down, and 6- to 10-inch stones form a border on the edges. Watch for short, numbered interpretive markers. Yucca plants, with their sword-like leaves, are scattered in the openings under the cedar trees.

Reach the Y where Shady Creek joins Cedar Flats, and take the left branch. This 0.3-mile loop is the most difficult section of the hike and may be bypassed by continuing on Cedar Flats. Shady Creek has a natural surface, including limestone outcroppings. Continue following Shady Creek north, and then at the Y with Hillview, take the right branch, staying on Shady Creek, heading east and then south.

There is a multijunction at a wooden bridge. Cross the bridge and continue on Shady Creek. Follow the trail as it leads in and out of a creek bed. Continue along the creek bed until reaching a T with Cedar Flats. Take the left branch, heading east and then southeast back to the trailhead.

Miles and Directions

0.0   Start at the Yucca Trailhead heading west.

0.3   Reach a Y and take the right branch, heading southwest. The left branch is also the Yucca Trail and part of a small loop that leads back to the main trail.

0.5   Pass a dry creek bed on the right, approximately 40 feet away. Low limestone outcrops are on the right and left. Follow the trail as it takes a hard right, heading north.

1.0   Reach a junction where Cedar Flats Trail (an asphalt trail) crosses Yucca. Turn right, going east on Cedar Flats.

1.2   Reach a Y and take the left branch onto Shady Creek Trail, heading north. NOTE: The 0.3-mile Shady Creek Trail is rugged. This section may be eliminated by continuing southwest on Cedar Flats toward the trailhead.

1.3 Reach a Y and take the right branch east, staying on Shady Creek.

1.4 Continue a short distance and reach a junction. Cross the bridge and follow Shady Creek to the right (south). Follow the trail along a creek bed.

1.6 Reach a T where Shady Creek ends at Cedar Flats Trail (asphalt). Take the left branch, heading southeast back toward Yucca.

1.7 Reach the T with Yucca, and take the left branch, heading east, and backtrack to the trailhead.

1.9 Arrive back at the trailhead.

3 Stone Oak Park: Spider's Dare Trail

This relatively new park, which opened in 2006, is developing some short but very interesting trails. The area is prime karst territory, somewhat similar to the Hill Country. The entrances to Cub Cave and Bear Cave may be viewed. Interpretive signage adds interest to the hike. What hiker could resist a trail called "Spider's Dare"?

Distance: 1.2-mile clockwise loop

Approximate hiking time: 1 hour

Difficulty: Easy due to flat paved trail

Trail surface: Concrete aggregate

Best seasons: Sept–June

Other trail users: Joggers, dog walkers

Canine compatibility: Leashed dogs permitted

Land status: City park; San Antonio Parks and Recreation Department

Fees and permits: None required

Schedule: Dawn to dusk daily

Maps: Park map is on the kiosk at the trailhead. No other maps available. USGS Bulverde

Trail contacts: San Antonio Parks and Recreation, P.O. Box 839966, San Antonio 78283; (210) 207-3000; www.san antonio.gov/sapar

Finding the trailhead: From north of downtown, take US 281 to the I-1604 loop. Take I-1604 1.5 miles west to the Stone Oak Parkway exit. Exit onto Stone Oak Parkway and proceed north for 3.5 miles to 20395 Stone Oak Parkway. Turn left into the park entrance road and parking lot. The trailhead is adjacent to the parking lot. *DeLorme: Texas Atlas & Gazetteer:* Page 157 B7. GPS: N 29 38.817'/ W 98 28.170'

The Hike

There is a park map on the kiosk at the entrance. Information boards near the shelter tell about the flora, fauna, and geology of the area. Allow extra time to read the information at the numerous interpretive stops and to view the varied small iron sculptures. The sculptures are made from "pre-rusted" iron, attempting to be less obtrusive to the natural background.

After heading west from the trailhead, almost immediately pass a low stone wall, off the trail and on the right. Closer inspection reveals that the wall circles the entrance to Cub Cave. This is one of several karst caves in the region that allow water to flow down through limestone channels to the Edwards Aquifer. Entry is not permitted. The Edwards Aquifer is the primary source of water for San Antonio.

In about 600 feet (two football fields), reach an interpretive sign, with a schematic for Bear Cave. The cave is home to a colony of bats living in the "Bat Room," which is 36 feet in diameter, 26 feet high, and covered with guano (bat droppings). The cave entrance is surrounded by a low stone wall, and the entrance proper is covered by a grate, allowing the bats and other wildlife access.

Make a hard right after 0.2 mile, heading north. A gravel road is ahead on the left and blocked by a gate. Continue north and see some large mansions on the hill ahead and to the left. After 0.3 mile reach the first of several interpretive stations. This one tells about armadillos, claiming some people eat them and they taste like pork. Some of the interpretive stations have benches near them.

Bear right (southeast) and follow the trail until it bends sharply to the right and heads south. This goes past portions

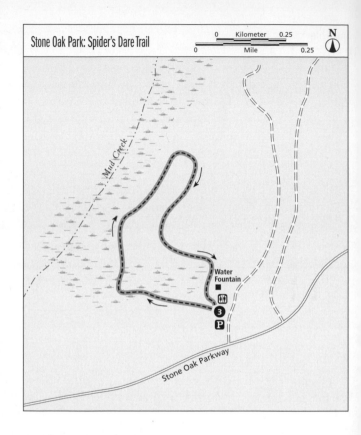

Stone Oak Park: Spider's Dare Trail

Kilometer 0.25

Mile 0.25

N

Mud Creek

Water Fountain

3

Stone Oak Parkway

of the previous section of trail. Watch for "Swiss cheese" rocks on both sides. These are rocks with holes in them, resembling Swiss cheese, and can be from fist size to boulder size. Reach interpretive stations about every 0.1 mile. Most have small iron sculptures placed on top of a rock base.

Follow Spider's Dare, turning right and then left, heading generally south. Then make a hard left, going east for a short distance, and then make a hard right, going south. Follow the trail past Cub Cave and back to the trailhead.

Miles and Directions

0.0 Start at the Spider's Dare Trail trailhead, heading west.

0.1 In less than 300 feet, pass a low stone wall on the right, about 15 feet from the trail. The wall circles the entry to Cub Cave. Entry to the cave is prohibited.

0.15 Pass a path on the right that leads to a low stone wall, about 25 feet from the trail. The wall circles the entry to Bear Cave. Entry to the cave is prohibited.

0.2 Turn right, following the trail north. On the left is a narrow gravel road blocked by a gate.

0.3 Reach an interpretive station on the right. Pass a small, concrete, semicircular area bordered by rocks with a bench.

0.4 Reach an interpretive station that explains the yellow stonecrop plant. There is a sit-up bench exercise station nearby.

0.5 Pass a trail that comes in from the right. It is a shortcut back to the trailhead. Continue following Spider's Dare.

0.6 Reach an interpretive station on the right. Continue on Spider's Dare.

0.7 Follow the trail on a semicircle that goes from north to south, and continue south. In about 200 feet, reach an interpretive station. There is an exercise station for push-ups nearby. Follow the trail as it bears left (east), then makes a hard right, going south.

0.9 Pass a trail coming from the right. It is the end of the shortcut passed at 0.5 mile. Almost immediately reach a bench and interpretive station on the right, telling about the Virginia opossum.

1.0 Reach an interpretive station on the right, telling about the prickly pear cactus.

1.1 Reach a Y and take the left branch, heading south. The right branch leads to Cub Cave. Continue following the trail to the trailhead.

1.2 Arrive back at the trailhead.

4 Crownridge Canyon Natural Area: Red Oak Trail

Red Oak Trail winds through a forested area in this 207–acre park. It crosses a bridge overlooking Red Oak Canyon and then completes the loop back at the trailhead. Along the trail's edge, interpretive markers that identify flora add interest to the hike.

Distance: 1.3-mile clockwise loop
Approximate hiking time: 1 hour
Difficulty: Easy due to paved, shaded trail
Trail surface: Stabilized concrete road mix
Best seasons: Year-round
Other trail users: Bird-watchers
Canine compatibility: Dogs not permitted
Land status: San Antonio natural area park; San Antonio Parks and Recreation Department
Fees and permits: None required

Schedule: 7:30 a.m. to sunset daily; closed Christmas and New Year's Day
Maps: Trail maps are available on the Web site www.sannatural areas.org; USGS Helotes
Trail contacts: Friedrich Wilderness Park, 21395 Milsa Rd., San Antonio 78256; (210) 564-6400. NOTE: Friedrich is headquarters for natural areas.
Special considerations: Bicycles not allowed

Finding the trailhead: From northwest San Antonio, take I-10 west about 0.5 mile past Loop 1604. Then take exit 554 for Camp Bullis Road. Stay on the access road and go about 2 miles and take a left, going under I-10 onto Camp Bullis Road, heading west. Proceed 1.6 miles to Luskey Boulevard, turn right, and follow to 7222 Luskey Blvd. Then turn right into the entrance of Crownridge. The trailhead is adjacent to the parking lot. Crownridge is about 19 miles

The Hike

Take time to read the information boards at the trailhead, next to the pavilion, telling about the flora and fauna found in the park. There is a kiosk with a large park map. There is an interesting rainwater harvesting demonstration, showing rainwater being collected from the pavilion roof. Restroom facilities and water are available at the trailhead. The trail is wheelchair and stroller accessible and has good signage.

Head north for a short distance and reach some limestone steps going up about 5 feet and surrounded by shrubs and flowers. Here the trail makes an acute left turn, heading west for a very short distance. Then make a hard right and head north. Some snakes call the park home, including the nonvenomous hognose and green snakes and the venomous copperhead.

Continue following the trail north with some minor turns right and left. Benches are placed along the sides of the trail, some in good shade. Watch for ball moss attached to some of the tree limbs. Most of the mammals found in the park are nocturnal or elusive. These include raccoon, coyote, fox, skunk, bobcats, and ring-tailed cats. Watch for white-tailed deer, rabbits, and squirrels during the day.

About 0.5 mile from the trailhead, reach the Red Oak Canyon Bridge. Good views of the shallow canyon are available. Make a hard right, heading east, then make a semicircle and head north. Reach the Y with the Bear Grass Trail. Take the right branch, heading east for a short distance, and then make a hard right, heading south, and pass the junction with Bear Grass Trail.

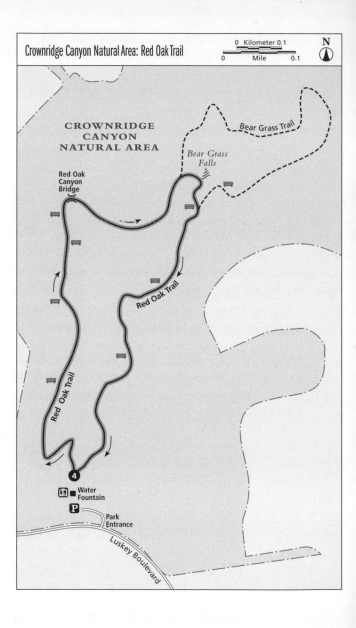

Crownridge Canyon Natural Area: Red Oak Trail

0   Kilometer 0.1

0   Mile   0.1

N

CROWNRIDGE
CANYON
NATURAL AREA

Bear Grass Trail

Bear Grass
Falls

Red Oak
Canyon
Bridge

Red Oak Trail

Red Oak Trail

4

Water
Fountain

P

Park
Entrance

Luskey Boulevard

Continue following Red Oak generally south, with zigs and zags to the right and left. Pass a habitat reforestation area that has various types of enclosures protecting small plants and trees from browsing deer. The deer have devastated much of the cedar, elm, red oak, and wild cherry. Watch for live oak, Texas persimmon, and prickly pear cactus. Some of the cactus appears to be growing out of a limestone outcrop, making a good photo op.

The trail parallels an unnamed creek (why not Red Oak?) on the left side that flows through Red Oak Canyon. There are 15- to 20-foot drop-offs to the creek. Hardwood trees, with a few cedars mixed in, fill the canyon. Continue traveling south on the trail and then bear right back to the trailhead.

Miles and Directions

0.0 Start at the trailhead of Red Oak Trail.

0.1 Reach limestone steps and follow the trail as it doubles back on itself. Continue following the trail north for a short distance, then make a hard left, heading southeast, then make a hard right, heading north.

0.5 Reach the Red Oak Canyon Bridge. Cross the bridge and follow the trail, bending hard right and going southeast and then left heading northeast.

0.6 Large residences can be seen on a hill about 0.5 mile away.

0.8 Reach a T and take the right branch, heading west. The left branch is Bear Grass Trail. Follow Red Oak a short distance and then make a hard right, heading south.

0.9 Pass a dry creek bed and gully on the left.

1.0 Pass a bench on the left and then cross a concrete bridge over a creek. Interpretive marker 62 is on the right. This creek has formed Red Oak Canyon. Continue following the trail south toward the trailhead.

1.3 Arrive back at the trailhead.

5 Comanche Lookout Park: Loop and Lookout Tower Trails

The 92-acre Comanche Lookout Park has a wealth of history. The Loop Trail has been combined with the Comanche Lookout Tower Trail to explore the most interesting sections of the park. The four-story medieval-style stone tower sitting on top of the 1,340-foot-high hill is the high point of the hike. Portions of the paved trail are wheelchair and stroller accessible.

Distance: 1.7-mile double loop
Approximate hiking time: 1.5 hours
Difficulty: Moderate due to fairly long grades up
Trail surface: Asphalt, concrete, gravel
Best seasons: Year-round
Other trail users: Joggers, dog walkers
Canine compatibility: Leashed dogs permitted
Land status: Bexar County park; San Antonio Parks and Recreation Department
Fees and permits: None required
Schedule: Dawn to dusk daily
Maps: Large park map on kiosk at trailhead. You can also find maps on the Web site, www.san antonio.gov/sapar; USGS Schertz
Trail contacts: San Antonio Parks and Recreation, P.O. Box 839966, San Antonio 78283; (210) 207-3000; www.san antonio.gov/sapar

Finding the trailhead: From northeast of downtown, take I-410 east to Judson Road. Exit at Judson Road and proceed north for 2 miles to Nacogdoches Road. Turn right (east) onto Nacogdoches Road and proceed 0.5 mile to 15551 Nacogdoches Road. Turn left into the park entrance and parking lot. The trailhead is adjacent to the parking lot. *DeLorme: Texas Atlas & Gazetteer:* Page 157 C12. GPS: N 29 34.965' / W 98 22.009'

The Hike

Spend some time at the pavilion reading about the park history. This area was used by the Apache and Comanche Indians during the eighteenth and nineteenth centuries. Cibolo Creek attracted many animals and furnished fertile hunting grounds for the Indians. One of the routes of El Camino Real, the Spanish Royal Road going from San Antonio to Bastrop, went past the hill. Remnants of some of these trails form part of Nacogdoches Road. The hill also furnished the Apaches and Comanches with a lookout to view and then attack mule trains and travelers.

Head north for a short distance and reach the intersection with the east side of the Loop Trail. Follow the Loop Trail left (west) and then bend right, heading north when the intersections of the Small Loop Trail on the left have been passed. The park encompasses sections of the Gulf Coast Plain and the Edwards Plateau ecosystems, so vegetation is varied. Good canopy is furnished by numerous trees, including cedar, Texas and Mexican buckeye, mesquite, and others. During the spring there is a profusion of wildflowers, including daisies.

After about 0.25 mile, pass an intersection on the right, which is a shortcut to the north side of the Loop Trail. Continue following the trail north past some subdivisions on the left, and then bear right, heading southeast. Pass the intersection where the shortcut mentioned at 0.25 mile dead-ends into the Loop Trail. Stay on the Loop Trail, head east, and then make a semicircle to the right and head south to the junction with the Lookout Tower Trail. Follow the Lookout Tower Trail to the Comanche Lookout Tower. The four-story tower, resembling medieval towers

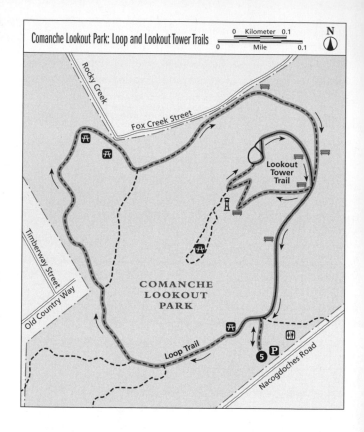

Comanche Lookout Park: Loop and Lookout Tower Trails

0   Kilometer   0.1

0   Mile   0.1

N

Rocky Creek

Fox Creek Street

Lookout
Tower
Trail

COMANCHE
LOOKOUT
PARK

Timberway Street

Old Country Way

Loop Trail

5 P

Nacogdoches Road

in Europe, is surrounded by a fence, and entry is prohibited. There is a water fountain located here.

Retired Army Colonel Edward H. Coppock purchased this property in 1923 from German immigrants who had farmed the land. Prior to his death in 1948, Coppock, who was a history buff, completed the tower and some other ceremonial-type structures. He had hoped to build an historical compound, including a castle. The tower is all that remains.

Take the trail going north from the tower and follow it as it bears right, heading south, until reaching the junction with the Loop Trail. Take the Loop Trail branch to the right, and follow it south to the trailhead.

Miles and Directions

0.0 Start at the Loop Trail trailhead, adjacent to the parking lot, and head north, away from Nacogdoches Road.

0.1 Reach the intersection with the east side of the Loop Trail. Turn left, heading west on the paved trail.

0.2 Reach the Y with the Small Loop Trail. Take the right branch, staying on the Loop Trail and heading north.

0.25 Reach a Y and take the left branch, heading slightly northwest. The right branch is a shortcut to the north side of the Loop Trail.

0.6 Continue following the Loop Trail, bearing to the right and passing a subdivision on the left. Make a hard right, heading southeast and away from the road and subdivision.

0.7 Follow a slight slope up to a Y and take the left branch, heading east. The right branch is the junction with the shortcut from 0.25 mile.

0.8 A path comes in from the left from the parking lot at the Fox Run Elementary School. Continue heading east on the Loop Trail.

1.0 After following the trail in a wide semicircle and then heading south, reach a Y. Take the left branch heading west toward Comanche Lookout Tower. Follow the trail as it makes a hard right and an immediate hard left.

1.3 Reach the Comanche Lookout Tower. Follow the trail northeast; it then curves to the south.

1.5 Reach the junction with the Loop Trail. Continue to the right and head south to the trailhead.

1.7 Arrive back at the trailhead.

6 Friedrich Wilderness Park: Main Loop, Vista Loop, and Fern Del Trail

Perched high on the Balcones Escarpment, this hike becomes exhilarating on the short Fern Del Trail. Go up steep limestone outcroppings, called steps, through a dwarf forest and along a singletrack, cliff-hugging path overlooking the canyon. Vista Loop offers a glimpse of the San Antonio skyline. Follow segments of the Main Loop, Vista Loop, Fern Del, and Water Trails to get the best of Friedrich.

Distance: 2.3-mile lollipop

Approximate hiking time: 1.75 hours

Difficulty: Easy except for the 0.25-mile Fern Del Trail, which is more challenging due to steep inclines over limestone outcrops

Trail surface: Concrete, wood chips, limestone outcrops, dirt path

Best seasons: Sept through June

Other trail users: Joggers

Canine compatibility: Dogs not permitted

Land status: San Antonio natural area park; San Antonio Parks and Recreation Department

Fees and permits: No fees or permits required

Schedule: 8:00 a.m. to 5:00 p.m. Oct through March; 8:00 a.m. to 8:00 p.m. Apr through Sept; closed Christmas Day and New Year's Day. Park entrance closes one hour before closing time.

Maps: A trail map is available in the park office. A map is also on the Web at www.sannaturalareas .org. USGS Camp Bullis

Trail contacts: Friedrich Wilderness Park, 21395 Milsa Rd., San Antonio 78256; (210) 564-6400. NOTE: Friedrich is headquarters for natural areas.

Finding the trailhead: From downtown San Antonio, take I-10 west about 0.5 mile past Loop 1604. Take exit 554 for Camp Bullis Road; this is the second exit past Loop 1604. Go 2 miles on the access road, take a left under the interstate, and an immediate right on the (two-way) access road. Proceed 2 miles to Oak Drive and turn left. At the end of Oak Drive, turn right onto Milsa Road. Friedrich Wilderness Park is on your left at 21480 Milsa Rd. Follow the entrance road to the left to the parking lot and trailhead. *DeLorme: Texas Atlas & Gazetteer:* Page 68 K6. GPS: N 29 38.454' / W 98 37.541'

The Hike

Start at the Main Loop trailhead, located near the sidewalk adjacent to the parking lot. Pick up a trail map at the sign-in stand near the restrooms. This hike combines sections of the Main Loop, Vista Loop, Fern Del Trail, and Water Trail to view the contrast between the flat valleys, dwarf forests, and limestone *balcones* found in the park.

In a short distance the trail branches; follow the right branch, which makes a right turn, going north. The concrete surface ends at a three-way branch. Follow the right branch, which is the northern section of the Main Loop.

The trail heads upward and, during a steep climb, passes through a dwarf forest containing mainly Ashe's juniper and blackjack oak. At the top there is a Y branch; take the left leg, heading west on the Vista Loop.

Almost immediately there is another branch; go left onto the Fern Del Trail, which is the most exhilarating and strenuous part of the hike. There are steep ascents and descents over limestone outcroppings that the park calls steps. The short trail loop starts at the bottom of a north-facing canyon, then climbs about 200 feet to near the top of the canyon and back down. Complete the Fern Del loop at

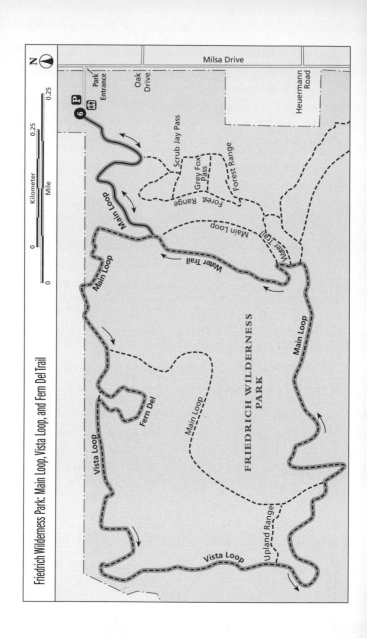

Friedrich Wilderness Park: Main Loop, Vista Loop, and Fern Del Trail

N

Kilometer
0   0.25
0   0.25
Mile

Milsa Drive

Park Entrance
Oak Drive
Heuermann Road

Scrub Jay Pass
Grey Fox Pass
Forest Range
Forest Range
Main Loop
Water Trail
Water Trail
Main Loop

Main Loop
Main Loop

Main Loop

FRIEDRICH WILDERNESS PARK

Fern Del
Vista Loop

Upland Range
Vista Loop

a T, where it ends and connects with the Vista Loop. Take the left branch, heading west on Vista Loop. On a clear day San Antonio can be seen from the overlooks.

Much of the trail follows narrow rock ledges as it passes through woodlands dominated by lacey oak, along with Spanish oak, cherry, and walnut. The trail then branches, with the left branch being the Upland Range connector to the Main Loop. A low, stacked limestone wall crosses the trail; what its use was is a matter of conjecture.

The Vista Loop ends when it connects to the Main Loop. Take the right branch, heading south on the Main Loop. Continue on the Main Loop to where it meets the Water Trail and go left.

Highlights on the trail before reaching the windmill are an intermittent creek and a large, seasonal spring. The section to the windmill is narrow and sometimes difficult. The windmill is one of the oldest working windmills in Bexar County. Then continue north to meet the concrete section of the Main Loop. Follow the right branch and backtrack to the trailhead.

Miles and Directions

0.0   Start at the Main Loop trailhead just off the parking lot.

0.1   Pass the Forest Range connector on the left (south). Continue on the Main Loop, making a right bend heading north.

0.3   The Main Loop connector trail T branches with the north and south sections of the Main Loop and connects with the Water Trail. Turn hard right and head north on the Main Loop.

0.6   There is a Y branch where Main Loop and Vista Loop join. Turn right (west) onto Vista Loop. Within less than 0.1 mile, you'll come to where Fern Del Trail intersects Vista Loop on the left (south). Turn left, heading south onto Fern Del. This is a steep, rugged trail. This is the most difficult part of the hike. You can bypass this section by continuing on Vista Loop at the intersection.

0.8 The Fern Del Trail intersects with Vista Loop and ends. Turn left and head west on Vista Loop.

1.05 Make a sharp left turn, heading south.

1.3 Pass the Upland Range connector trail to the Main Loop on the left (east).

1.6 The Vista Loop T's into and ends at the Main Loop. Take the right (south) leg of the Main Loop.

2.0 Take a hard left, heading north on the Main Loop where the Juniper Barrens Trail intersects and ends at the Main Loop. Follow the Main Loop north for a very short distance to where the Water Trail intersects the Main Loop on the left (southwest). Turn hard left onto the Water Trail and go southeast.

2.2 The Water Trail ends, joining the Main Loop at a Y branch. Take the right leg of the Main Loop and backtrack to the trailhead.

2.3 Arrive back at the trailhead.

7 Government Canyon State Natural Area: Savannah Loop

The Savannah Loop in the frontcountry of Government Canyon State Natural Area is one of the tamer trails in this state natural area. This is a good hike for families. The trail parallels Government Canyon Creek for the first third, and then goes through meadows and woods. A mix of single- and doubletrack sections adds interest to the hike.

Distance: 2.3-mile lollipop loop
Approximate hiking time: 1.2 hours
Difficulty: Easy due to mostly even terrain
Trail surface: Dirt path; a few rocky areas
Best seasons: Sept through June
Other trail users: Mountain bikers, dog walkers, trail runners
Canine compatibility: Leashed dogs permitted but are restricted to the frontcountry trails
Land status: State natural area; Texas Parks & Wildlife Department
Fees and permits: Fee required, or use the State Parks Pass. A trail permit is required.
Schedule: Open 8:00 a.m. to 6:00 p.m. Friday through Monday (closed Tuesday through Thursday). Access to backcountry trails closes at 4:00 p.m.; access to frontcountry trails closes at 5:00 p.m. Protected Habitat Area trails close March 1 to Sept. 1. Laurel Canyon Trail is closed.
Maps: Trail maps are available in the park office. You can also find maps on the Web site www.tpwd .state.tx.us; USGS Helotes
Trail contacts: Government Canyon State Natural Area, 12861 Galm Rd., San Antonio 78254; (210) 688-9055
Special considerations: Prior to going to the Government Canyon State Natural Area, contact the park for information about trails that may be closed due to inclement weather or poor trail conditions.

Finding the trailhead: From Loop 1604 in San Antonio, go 3.5 miles west on FR 471 to Galm Road and turn right (north). Travel for about 1.5 miles to the park entrance at 12861 Galm Rd. *DeLorme: Texas Atlas & Gazetteer:* Page 77 B11. GPS (park headquarters): N 29 55.276' / W 98 74.429'

The Hike

Follow the feeder trail at the back of parking lot C, using the multiuse trailhead that leads to the Savannah Loop. Be sure to follow the brown carsonite trail markers with the grass symbol pointing in the direction of the start of the trail. The trail is located in the section of the natural area known as the frontcountry.

Continue on the flat, gently rolling terrain and look for animal tracks, including those of the coyote, which are residents. The amount of wildlife in the area has earned the natural area recognition as HOTE 085 on the Heart of Texas Wildlife Trail. After passing trail marker 4, head northeast, away from the creek, to a left bend where the trail heads north.

Prickly pear cactus, some cedar elms, and mesquite are scattered in the woods. It's possible to see an eastern hog-nose snake near the trail; they will huff and puff and spread their necks to resemble a cobra. They are harmless and put on an interesting show. Stay on the trail, for venomous western diamondback rattlesnakes also inhabit the park, but they really try to avoid people. You're more likely to see squirrels, cottontail rabbits, and wild pigs. The wild pigs usually travel in groups, and the tusks growing out of their mouths help them present a ferocious image. They take cover if startled by people.

Nearly three-fourths of the park lies north of the fault

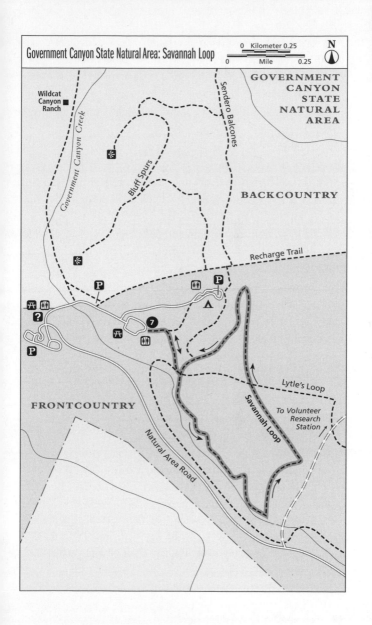

Government Canyon State Natural Area: Savannah Loop

0   Kilometer   0.25
0   Mile   0.25

N

Wildcat
Canyon
Ranch

Government Canyon Creek

Sendero Balcones

GOVERNMENT
CANYON
STATE
NATURAL
AREA

Bluff Spurs

BACKCOUNTRY

Recharge Trail

7

Lytle's Loop

Savannah Loop

To Volunteer
Research
Station

FRONTCOUNTRY

Natural Area Road

line that makes up one of the largest karst preserves in the country. A karst is where groundwater seeps into an aquifer through sinkholes and fractures in limestone, in this case filling the Edwards Aquifer.

Lytle's Loop intersects the Savannah Loop. Continue straight (north) on Savannah Loop. Wild turkey and hawks can frequently be seen here. Patches of mountain laurel grow along this corridor.

The trail narrows a bit and then enters a wooded area that has some open meadows where bluebonnets, the state flower, Indian paintbrush, and other wildflowers can be seen from March through May. Birds like this area; depending on the time of year, cardinals, painted buntings, and summer tanagers may be seen.

The trail makes a sharp turn to the left, and the direction abruptly changes from north to southwest. The loop ends at trail marker 1, where you backtrack on the feeder trail to the parking lot.

Miles and Directions

- **0.0** Start at the trailhead for Savannah Loop.
- **0.5** Head south to reach trail marker 4.
- **0.9** Travel northeast to reach trail marker 7.
- **1.3** Travel north to reach trail marker 9; the trail changes to a wider path. Reach the intersection of Lytle's Loop. Continue straight (north) on Savannah Loop.
- **2.1** Continue north to where the trail makes a sharp turn southwest. End the loop at trail marker 1 and backtrack on the feeder trail.
- **2.3** End the Savannah Loop hike and arrive back at the trailhead and parking lot C.

8 Government Canyon State Natural Area: Bluff Spurs Trail

Imagine an area ten times as large as New York City's Central Park with 36 miles of trails . . . that's Government Canyon State Natural Area. Walk on the geological fault that separates the Edwards Plateau and the blackland prairie ecosystem. Scramble down steep limestone outcrops, mis-leadingly called steps. View 80-foot canyon walls created by Government Creek.

Distance: 3.2-mile loop, including the feeder trail from the trailhead
Approximate hiking time: 2 hours
Difficulty: Easy except for a few rocky uphill sections
Trail surface: Dirt; rocky lime-stone outcrop
Best seasons: Sept through June
Other trail users: None
Canine compatibility: Dogs not permitted anywhere in the back-country
Land status: State natural area, Texas Parks & Wildlife Depart-ment
Fees and permits: Fee required, or use the State Parks Pass. A trail permit is required.
Schedule: Open 8:00 a.m. to 6:00 p.m. Friday through Monday (closed Tuesday through Thurs-day). Access to backcountry trails closes at 4:00 p.m.; access to frontcountry trails closes at 5:00 p.m. Protected Habitat Area trails close March 1 to Sept 1. Laurel Canyon Trail is closed.
Maps: Trail maps are available in the park office. Maps also avail-able on the Web at www.tpwd .state.tx.us; USGS Helotes
Trail contacts: Government Can-yon State Natural Area, 12861 Galm Rd., San Antonio 78254; (210) 688-9055
Special considerations: Prior to going to Government Canyon State Natural Area, contact the park for information about trails that may be closed due to inclement weather or poor trail conditions.

Finding the trailhead: From Loop 1604 in San Antonio, go 3.5 miles west on FR 471 to Galm Road and turn right (north). Travel for about 1.5 miles to the park entrance at 12861 Galm Rd. Proceed to the park headquarters; the trailhead is to the east in parking lot D. *DeLorme: Texas Atlas & Gazetteer:* Page 77 B11. GPS (park headquarters): N 29 55.276' / W 98 74.429'

The Hike

Start the Bluff Spurs Trail at signpost 1 at the turnoff from Recharge Trail. Getting to the trailhead requires walking through an open meadow on Recharge Trail, which is on the fault that separates the blackland prairie and the Edwards Plateau.

Once on the Bluff Spurs Trail, start climbing uphill on the rocky singletrack. Be careful if it has recently rained, for the rocks can be slippery. Ashe's juniper, mountain laurel, and cedar elm woods form a welcome sun-shielding canopy overhead.

Those folks interested in geology will have a field day studying the exposed Edwards limestone. There are also excellent examples of karst limestone. The karst habitat lies beneath the surface of the plateau and is a honeycomb of caves, sinkholes, and springs.

Reach Bluff Spurs signpost 2, where the trail branches, and take the left branch, heading southwest toward the South Bluff Spurs Overlook. Just before the overlook, the trail is singletrack, very rocky, and has a few steep steps that lead down. The view is impressive, with hikers able to see the visitor center buildings and a couple of windmills. The trail dead-ends here among prickly pear cactus and large rocks that furnish a place to sit and rest.

Many mammals call the canyon home, among them

coyote, Virginia opossum, skunk, raccoon, bobcat, and white-tailed deer. Actually seeing them can be difficult, but you can add another dimension to the hike by taking along a field guide to animal tracks and trying to identify the various tracks around the trails. Seeing the print left by a bobcat's paw might give the hike a feel of backcountry adventure.

Backtrack to the Bluff Spurs intersection and continue straight (north), then follow a gentle left turn to Bluff Spurs signpost 4. The trail is singletrack, going through wooded areas and leading to the North Bluff Spurs Overlook, which is identified by North Spur signpost 2.

Backtrack a short distance to where you turned off to get to the overlook, and follow the trail until it dead-ends by intersecting with the Sendero Balcones Trail. This is an interesting section affectionately referred to by the park rangers as the "hog wallow," due to the large number of wild hogs usually seen here.

This last section of the route, on Sendero Balcones Trail, is a very steep downhill limestone staircase (not real stairs, but outcroppings of limestone rocks), which makes it scenic but strenuous. Fortunately there's a bench to rest on about halfway down. Continue to the Recharge Trail and back-track to the parking lot.

Miles and Directions

- **0.0** To get to the Bluff Spurs trailhead start at parking lot D, on the Recharge Trail, and head east.
- **0.3** Reach the branch with the connector to Bluff Spurs Trail. Turn left, heading north.
- **0.9** Reach the Bluff Spurs Trail at signpost 2. Turn left and head southwest.

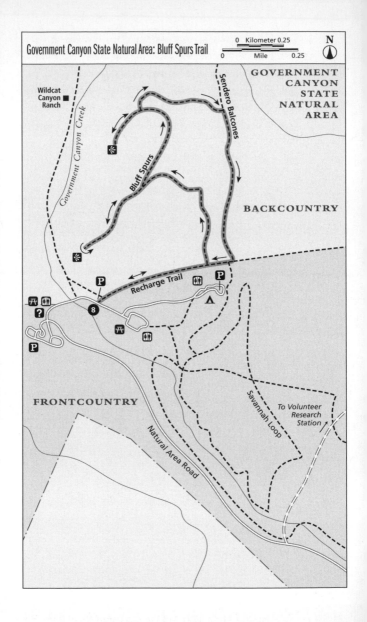

Government Canyon State Natural Area: Bluff Spurs Trail

0 Kilometer 0.25

0 Mile 0.25

N

GOVERNMENT CANYON STATE NATURAL AREA

Wildcat Canyon Ranch

Government Canyon Creek

Sendero Balcones

Bluff Spurs

BACKCOUNTRY

Recharge Trail

8

FRONTCOUNTRY

Natural Area Road

Savannah Loop

To Volunteer Research Station

1.3 Reach the South Bluff Spurs Overlook. This is an out-and-back section of the trail. Backtrack to signpost 2.

1.7 Reach signpost 2 and pass the connector trail on the right (east). Stay on the Bluff Spurs Trail, heading northeast.

2.0 Reach signpost 4, where the trail branches. Turn left, heading southwest, to the North Bluff Spurs Overlook.

2.2 Reach the overlook. The trail is singletrack just before the overlook. This is another out-and-back section. Backtrack to signpost 4.

2.4 The trail branches. Take the left branch, heading northeast.

2.7 The Bluff Spurs Trail intersects and dead-ends at the Sendero Balcones Trail. Turn right, heading south. The last half of this trail is a very steep downhill on limestone.

2.8 Reach the intersection with the Recharge Trail. Turn right (west) and follow the Recharge Trail to parking lot D.

3.2 Arrive back at the trailhead and parking lot D.

9 Bamberger Nature Park: Exercise Loop and Leon Creek Loop

This very small park offers two completely different walking experiences by combining the Exercise Loop and the Leon Creek Loop. The 0.4-mile paved, flat Exercise Loop provides a warm-up for the slightly longer Leon Creek trail. The Leon Creek Loop goes through the woods, and sections of it border the creek. The hike is suitable for families with young children.

Distance: 1.1-mile loop
Approximate hiking time: 1 hour
Difficulty: Easy due to some paved and most shaded trails
Trail surface: Concrete on Exercise trail; stone and rock on the Leon Creek Loop
Best seasons: Year-round
Other trail users: Joggers, dog walkers, bikers
Canine compatibility: Leashed dogs permitted
Land status: City park; San Antonio Parks and Recreation Department

Fees and permits: None required
Schedule: 6:00 a.m. to 10:00 p.m. daily
Maps: No maps available; USGS Helotes
Trail contacts: San Antonio Parks and Recreation, P.O. Box 839966, San Antonio 78283; (210) 207-3000; www.san antonio.gov/sapar
Special considerations: No restroom facilities or water are available in the park

Finding the trailhead: From northwest San Antonio, take I-410 west to the Babcock Road exit. Exit and follow Babcock Road 7 miles north to 12901 Babcock Rd. Turn into the parking lot. The trailhead is adjacent to the parking lot. *DeLorme: Texas Atlas & Gazetteer:* Page 156 E1. GPS: N 29 33.611' / W 98 37.796'

The Hike

A sign at the trailhead warns that this area is subject to flash flooding. In the event of rain, be prepared to reach higher ground. The Exercise Loop is a flat, asphalt oval. Start at the trailhead, which is a T connecting with the Leon Creek Loop. Head east and then continue bearing right around the loop until you arrive back at the trailhead. The vehicle sounds from Babcock Road and the residences, which are clearly in view, are a reminder that this is a city hike.

The trail goes through mixed hardwoods, shrubs, and wildflowers. This, combined with the nearness of Leon Creek, furnishes excellent habitat for wildlife, especially birds. Complete the Exercise Loop and continue north at the trailhead onto Leon Creek Loop. The tree canopy that furnishes shade is erratic, so wear a hat.

Follow the natural surface in and out of the woods. Hardy mesquite and cedar trees, along with other hardwoods, make up the woods. As the trail undulates up and down, a few low limestone outcrops cross it. Many narrow "biker paths" can be seen. Portions of the trail parallel Leon Creek, which can range from swift flowing to a dry creek bed, depending on the amount of rainfall.

There are numerous opportunities to follow one of the many "rogue" paths to the creek's edge and look for animal tracks. Prickly pear cactus and yucca can be seen in openings in the woods. About halfway through the hike, reach a T intersection, which has an information sign. This property was part of the Nantz Ranch, which operated from 1878 to 1984. The original owners were Juan and Laura De Sais Nantz. A large live oak shades the sign. From the sign, follow the trail southeast and then bear right, heading south–

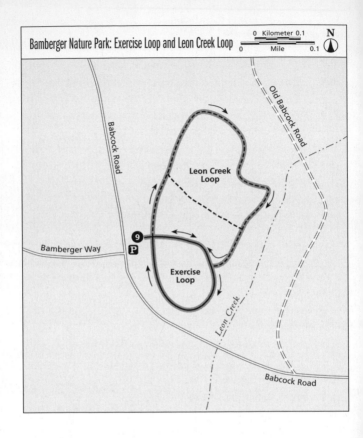

0 Kilometer 0.1

0   Mile   0.1

N

Babcock Road

Old Babcock Road

Leon Creek Loop

Bamberger Way

9

P

Exercise Loop

Leon Creek

Babcock Road

west. In less than 0.1 mile, turn right, heading west and back to the trailhead.

There are many paths created by bikers and "explorer" hikers. They lead in all directions into the woods, so stay on the main trail so as not to become disoriented. All the Leon Creek Loop branches are marked and bordered by five or six large boulders.

Miles and Directions

0.0 Start at the Exercise Loop trailhead and head east.

0.1 Follow the path going to the right in a clockwise direction, heading east, then south, and then north.

0.2 Reach a sidewalk on the left that leads to the road. Continue following the asphalt Exercise trail clockwise.

0.4 Arrive back at the trailhead and continue a short distance west on the gravel Leon Creek Loop and then follow the trail, making a hard right and going north.

0.5 Cross over Leon Creek, using flat rocks to walk on. Then immediately reach a Y bordered by five large rocks and take the left branch, still heading north.

0.6 Make a hard right turn at the junction, heading east for a short distance. A path on the left leads down to the creek bed.

0.7 Reach a T and take the right branch, heading south. A memorial sign identifies this property as having been part of the Nantz Ranch.

0.9 Reach a T and take the left branch, heading southwest.

1.0 Recross the creek that was crossed at 0.5 mile and backtrack to the trailhead.

1.1 Arrive back at the trailhead.

10 Brackenridge Park: Wilderness and Wildlife Trails

Combine portions of the Wilderness and Wildlife Trails to see the best Brackenridge offers. Nearly half the hike parallels the San Antonio River, allowing short out-and-backs to explore the river's edge. The trails are mostly shaded, paved, and flat, making them wheelchair and stroller accessible.

Distance: 1.4-mile clockwise loop

Approximate hiking time: 1 hour

Difficulty: Easy due to paved, shaded trails

Trail surface: Concrete, asphalt

Best seasons: Year-round

Other trail users: Joggers, dog walkers, bikers

Canine compatibility: Leashed dogs permitted

Land status: City park; San Antonio Parks and Recreation Department

Fees and permits: None required

Schedule: 6:00 a.m. to 10:00 p.m. daily

Maps: Maps available on the Internet at www.sanantonio.gov/sapar; USGS San Antonio East

Trail contacts: San Antonio Parks and Recreation, P.O. Box 839966, San Antonio 78283; (210) 207-3000; www.sanantonio.gov/sapar

Special considerations: Swimming in the San Antonio River is not allowed

Finding the trailhead: From downtown, take Broadway Street north to East Mulberry Avenue; turn left (west) at East Mulberry and proceed a few blocks to Avenue B. At Avenue B, turn right and follow to the parking area. The trailhead is adjacent to the parking area. *DeLorme: Texas Atlas & Gazetteer:* Page 159 A8. GPS: N 29 27.501' / W 98 28.262'

The Hike

This is San Antonio's most developed park, and as such it offers amenities not found on many hikes. These include a miniature train ride, a golf course, an adjoining zoo, playgrounds, and a Japanese tea garden. These can be enjoyed before or after the hike by both adults and children. All the trails are color-coded on the map; the trail signage is very good and also color-coded.

Check out the large park trail map mounted on the kiosk next to the Wilderness Trail trailhead. Also located there is the unique trailhead marker, a cartoon character standing on a 6-foot base made of rocks, water fountains, and a portable toilet that is within a partially enclosed stone structure. Head southwest and into the woods. Hardwood trees form a pleasant arch overhead. The edges of the trail are cleared and mowed.

Birds love this park with its woods and the San Antonio River as habitat. Take along a field guide on birds to add another dimension to the hike. In the winter watch for goldfinches passing through. These small yellow birds have a black patch on their forehead. Doves, robins, and white-throated sparrows are common.

Continue following the trail, generally southwest, as it passes several well-marked branches. Pass a large, cleared, circular area that has a display of short sections of tree trunks. In a short distance, and after passing several yucca plants, reach and cross a flat bridge over some wetlands. Then bear right, heading northwest, and cross Red Oak Road. Head north after crossing the road. This section runs parallel with the San Antonio River.

At this point the San Antonio is about 30 feet wide and

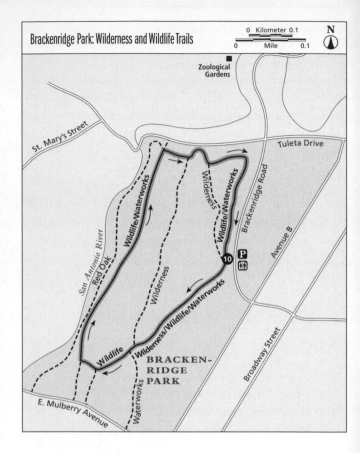

varies in depth, depending on the amount of rainfall. The edge of the river varies from being close to the edge of the trail to being 30 feet away. In the spring, parts of the river are filled with water lilies. A picnic area complete with tables and grills extends for nearly 0.25 mile along the river. The area is lighted and has large hardwood trees, including live oak, furnishing shade.

Near the end of the picnic area, make a hard right (northeast); for a short distance Tuleta Drive is on the left. Continue following the Wildlife Trail, and about 1 mile from the trailhead you'll reach a fantastic photo op. It is a huge tree trunk that is about 7 feet in diameter and cut off about 8 feet high. The inside has been hollowed out with a bench carved into it, and several windows have been cut out. Spectacular!

Wildlife Trail heads slightly southeast and then turns, going southwest, where it and Wilderness Trail are combined. Follow the trail back to the trailhead. This is one of the most relaxing and enjoyable hikes in San Antonio.

Miles and Directions

0.0 Start at the Wilderness Trail trailhead, identified by green markers, and head southwest.

0.1 Pass a dirt path coming from the woods on the right. Continue following the Wilderness Trail.

0.2 Reach a circular clearing with three trails branching from the circumference. Follow the circle around to the right and take the second trail. It is marked with an orange trail marker, indicating it is Wilderness Trail, and heads west.

0.3 Reach a Y and take the right branch, still heading west, onto the Wildlife Trail. Pass along a curving stone wall, about 4 feet high.

0.4 Reach a T just before Red Oak Road. Take the right branch, heading north. The San Antonio River is on the left.

0.6 Reach a trail marker with blue and orange identifiers and follow right, still heading north. The picnic area along the river is to the left, and Red Oak Road is on the right. Continue following the trail north.

0.9 Reach a large stone obelisk with a sign next to it with a large park map. Take a hard right, heading east, and cross Red

Oak Road. Use caution crossing the road. Tuleta Drive is on the left.

1.0 Follow the trail and make a hard right (south) as the trail approaches Brackenridge Road. Continue following the trail south back to the trailhead.

1.4 Arrive back at the trailhead.

11 Leon Creek Greenery: Buddy Calk Trail

The high point of this hike is enjoying the wildlife around the edge of the Earl Scott Pond. Birds can be heard in the creek valley and heavy woods. This is one of the new linear trails along the Leon Creek Greenery. It was opened in 2009 as part of the Linear Creekway program. It is wheelchair and stroller accessible.

Distance: 2.2-mile out-and-back
Approximate hiking time: 1.25 hour
Difficulty: Easy due to flat paved surface
Trail surface: Concrete, asphalt
Best seasons: Sept through June
Other trail users: Bikers, joggers, dog walkers
Canine compatibility: Leashed dogs permitted
Land status: City park; San Antonio Parks and Recreation Department

Fees and permits: None required
Schedule: 6:00 a.m. to 10:00 p.m. daily
Maps: Visit www.sanantonio .gov/creekways for maps; USGS Helotes
Trail contacts: San Antonio Parks and Recreation, P.O. Box 839966, San Antonio 78283; (210) 207-3000; www.san antonio.gov/sapar
Special considerations: Portable toilet and water fountain available at trailhead

Finding the trailhead: From northwest San Antonio, take I-410 west to the Babcock Road exit. Exit and follow Babcock Road 6.5 miles north to 12160 Babcock Rd. Turn into the parking lot. The trailhead is adjacent to the parking lot. *DeLorme: Texas Atlas & Gazetteer:* Page 156 E1. GPS: N 29 33.417' / W 98 37.604'

The Hike

The linear trail program utilizes areas adjacent to creeks and rivers that are generally part of a floodplain. They are wide, paved, multiuse trails and usually are out-and-back. Many of the segments have been connected, creating an opportunity to hike for a full day.

Start at the Buddy Calk trailhead near the shelter and water fountain. The trailhead is delineated by a group of boulders and small rocks bordered by a concrete ledge. Go under some power lines and pass a jeep maintenance road on the right. Continue following the sidewalk trail south. Residences may be seen over a fence about 150 feet on the left. The right side has woods. Leon Creek cannot be seen but is to the right.

In less than 0.3 mile reach the Earl Scott Pond. This is a large pond, and signs are posted stating that it has strong currents and swimming is not allowed. It is lined by willows and other trees, and there is a small beach area, suitable for picnics and wildlife watching. Several other paths lead down to the pond. Turtles may be seen sunning themselves on logs in the water. They usually slide into the water upon sensing vibrations from hikers walking. Watch for white-tailed deer in the early morning or around dusk. The edge of the pond is a good place to look for animal tracks. This is also a favorite spot for birds, especially in the woods on the west side.

Continue following the trail generally south around and past the pond. The residences on the left side of the trail are now closer and create some distraction. The tree canopy is open, and power lines from the Parkwood Subdivision cross overhead. Pass a trail marker post on the right indicating

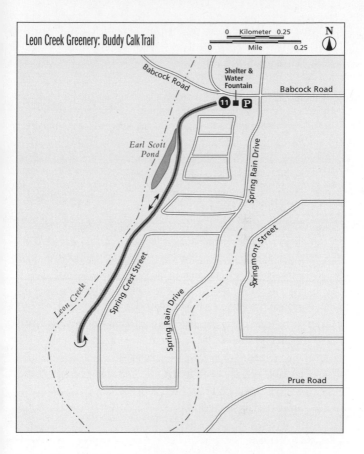

Leon Creek Greenery: Buddy Calk Trail

Babcock Road

Shelter & Water Fountain

Babcock Road

Earl Scott Pond

Spring Rain Drive

Springmont Street

Leon Creek

Spring Crest Street

Spring Rain Drive

Prue Road

O. P. Schnabel Park down the trail, while the left side has a concrete rest area. The rest area has an exit to the street and is to be used in the event of flash flooding.

The trail slopes slightly down and passes a concrete wall, about 18 inches high and 8 inches wide, on the left. It is suitable to sit on but is in the sun. Continue a short distance toward the Prue Road bridge, then backtrack to the trailhead. Those looking for more exercise can continue following the trail past Prue Road for several miles until it reaches O. P. Schnabel Park.

Miles and Directions

0.0 Start at the trailhead adjacent to the west end of the parking lot.

0.1 Make a hard left turn, heading south. A group of rocks bordered by a concrete edge is to the right.

0.3 Reach the Earl Scott Pond on the right. Continue following the trail south along the pond's edge.

0.6 Pass a gravel path on the right. The pond has ended. Overhead power lines are on the right.

0.7 A trail marker is on the right, and a rest area leading to the street is on the left. Continue nearly straight south, following the trail. NOTE: The exit to the street is to be used as a flood escape exit in the event of flash flooding.

0.75 Cross over a concrete drainage ditch. Continue straight south and then slightly southwest.

1.1 The trail changes to concrete, and the left side has a low concrete wall about 18 inches high. This is a good spot to rest and then backtrack to the trailhead.

2.2 Arrive back at the trailhead.

12 O. P. Schnabel Park: Leon Creek Vista Trail

The Leon Creek Vista Trail is the premier hike within the park's 200 acres and nearly 5 miles of trails. It passes through heavy cedar woods to reach the bluff overlooking Leon Creek and its valley. Many species of birds call the park home. Sections of the trail are wheelchair and stroller accessible.

Distance: 1.2-mile counterclockwise loop

Approximate hiking time: 1 hour

Difficulty: Easy due to paved trail

Trail surface: Asphalt, concrete

Best seasons: Year-round

Other trail users: Dog walkers, joggers, bikers

Canine compatibility: Leashed dogs permitted

Land status: City park; San Antonio Parks and Recreation Department

Fees and permits: None required

Schedule: Dawn to dusk daily

Maps: No maps available; USGS Helotes

Trail contacts: San Antonio Parks and Recreation, P.O. Box 839966, San Antonio 78283; (210) 207-3000; www.san antonio.gov/sapar

Finding the trailhead: From northwest San Antonio, take I-410 west to the TX 16 exit (Bandera Road). Take the exit, head north for 4.5 miles to 9600 Bandera Rd., and turn right onto the park road. Continue on the park entrance road past the YMCA facility on the left. Turn left at the stop sign and then into the parking area by the pavilion. The trailhead is on the northeast side of the parking lot. *DeLorme: Texas Atlas & Gazetteer:* Page 157 H10. GPS: N 29 32.138' / W 98 38.440'

The Hike

The park has ample drinking fountains and benches. Portions of the trail are lighted. It boasts two pavilions. The first, the Sadie Ray and Waldo Graf Pavilion, near the trailhead, is a large building that contains tables, benches, restroom facilities, and water fountains. The second is unnamed and along the trail. There are also playgrounds, basketball courts, and a YMCA facility available. The tree canopy is erratic, so wear a cap and use sunscreen.

Head east from the trailhead into the cedar woods. In less than 0.1 mile, pass a sidewalk leading to picnic tables and a water fountain. The paved trail slopes slightly uphill. Watch for wildlife in the woods near the edges of the trail. White-tailed deer may be seen early in the morning or around dusk. Continue following the trail east until it bends sharply left as it climbs to the bluffs above the Leon Creek Valley.

Reach a sidewalk on the right that leads to the vista above Leon Creek. There is a barricade there to help prevent people slipping over. The overlook is about 30 feet up. Paths lead down to the creek. This is the scenic high point of the hike. The park is alive with many species of birds; some can be heard or seen from here. Be extremely cautious! A hiker fell over the edge in 2009 and was killed. Return to the trail and head north.

Follow the trail north along the top of the bluffs. In places the cedar trees form an arch above the trail, creating pleasant shade from the Texas sun. Butterflies are common in the spring and summer, gathering nectar from the wildflowers. About 0.8 mile from the trailhead make a hard left and head west. The section runs along the park boundary, and residences, behind fences, are close on the right side.

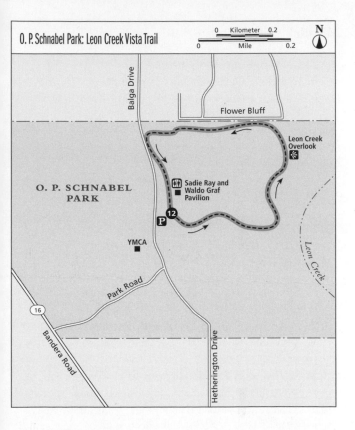

O. P. SCHNABEL PARK

Reach the park gate and turn left, following the park road back to the trailhead.

In addition to its hiking and mountain bike trails, the park has entered into the San Antonio Linear Creekway Program, which connects mostly out-and-back hikes along creeks and rivers. Access to the Leon Creek Greenery–Buddy Calk Trail can be made from O. P. Schnabel. The park is also listed as HOTE 91 on the Texas Parks & Wildlife Department maps, showing good viewing areas for birds and other wildlife.

The park was originally named Bandera Road Park but was renamed the O. P. Schnabel Park in 1977. Schnabel was known for his antilitter campaigns, especially for the slogans he created, including "Nice People Don't Litter" and "Be a Beauty Bug, Not a Litter Bug."

Miles and Directions

0.0 Start at the trailhead near the Sadie Ray and Waldo Graf Pavilion, heading east.

0.1 Pass a sidewalk on the left leading to a picnic table and water fountain. A dirt bike path is close by on the left.

0.2 Pass a portable toilet on the left, and in a short distance reach an open pavilion with a sheet-metal roof. Concrete benches, tables, fire grills, and a water fountain are at the pavilion.

0.3 Reach a concrete path on the right that leads to the Leon Creek Vista. The path loops back to the trail. Follow the trail north from the vista.

0.5 Reach a power transmission tower surrounded by a high chain-link fence.

0.6 A narrow dirt bike path is on the right. A trail marker sign identifies the difficulty levels assigned to trails.

0.8 Follow the trail, bearing hard left, heading west. Residences can be seen through the trees near the right edge of the trail.

1.0 Still following the trail west, reach the park gate. Turn left at the gate and head south along the park road. Continue south along the park road, passing some basketball courts across the road.

1.1 Pass the Graf Pavilion and proceed to the trailhead.

1.2 Arrive back at the trailhead.

13 Tobin Park: Oakwell Trail

This hike is for those who enjoy open woods filled with large (4-foot diameter), mature live oaks and other hardwoods. Some folks may remember playing in this type of woods when they were children. Salado Creek is within view for much of the way. The trail is wheelchair and stroller accessible.

Distance: 1.4-miles out and back

Approximate hiking time: 1 hour

Difficulty: Easy due to flat, shaded, paved trail

Trail surface: Asphalt

Best seasons: Year-round

Other trail users: Dog walkers, bikers, joggers

Canine compatibility: Leashed dogs permitted

Land status: City park; San Antonio Parks and Recreation Department

Fees and permits: None required

Schedule: 6:00 a.m. to 10:00 p.m. daily

Maps: Visit www.sanantonio.gov/ creekways for maps. No maps available in the park; USGS San Antonio East

Trail contacts: San Antonio Parks and Recreation, P.O. Box 839966, San Antonio 78283; (210) 207-3000; www.san antonio.gov/sapar

Special considerations: Smoking only in designated areas. There is a portable toilet adjacent to the parking lot. Swimming or wading is not allowed in Salado Creek.

Finding the trailhead: From north of downtown, take I-35 north to the Eisenhauer Road exit. Proceed west on Eisenhauer Road for 1.75 miles to Austin Highway. Turn right onto Austin Highway, proceed north about 0.5 mile, and turn onto Ira Lee Road. Follow Ira Lee for a few blocks to 100 Ira Lee Rd. Turn right into the park entrance and parking lot. The trailhead is adjacent to the parking lot. *DeLorme: Texas Atlas & Gazetteer:* Page 157 I10. GPS: N 29 30.136' / W 98 25.243'

The Hike

The Salado Creek Greenway is part of the San Antonio Linear Creekway Program, which connects mostly out-and-back hikes along creeks and rivers. It utilizes areas adjacent to creeks and rivers that are generally part of a floodplain. They are wide, paved, multiuse trails. Many of the segments have been connected, creating an opportunity to hike for a full day.

Check out the large display board at the trailhead, which contains a large park map and information about the flora and fauna within the park. This is a multiuse trail, so keep to the right and be aware of other people, especially bikers. Once on the trail and heading northeast, almost immediately cross two concrete bridges over a wet area. The woods contain many large hardwoods that have blocked much of the understory growth, so the trees have "open" areas around them. Most of the trail has an excellent tree canopy.

Salado Creek is to the right and can be seen for much of the hike. A group of residences are to the left, past a fence. The creek and mature trees create great habitat for wildlife, including a variety of birds. Listen and watch for cardinals, blue jays, and the colorful ladder-backed woodpecker. Doves like the area, and if a group of them takes off, they can even startle a seasoned hiker. Southern pecan trees are mixed with the live oak and other hardwoods in the forest. Watch for white-tailed deer among the trees during early morning or around dusk.

In the spring and fall, butterflies, including the painted lady, may be seen. Numerous climbing vines use the trees for support, and there are patches of poison ivy along the edge of the trail. Continue following the trail, bearing

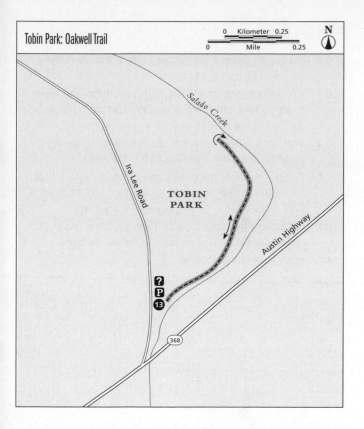

slightly left (northwest). Pass a trail marker showing the distance to the Tobin trailhead and the Oakwell trailhead. After a short distance, reach a large live oak with branches that cross above the trail. From this point backtrack to the trailhead.

The Tobin Endowment donated the land for the Robert Tobin Park. The land was once part of Oakwell, a 500-acre horse farm and home of the Tobin family.

Miles and Directions

0.0 Start at the Oakwell Trail trailhead adjacent to the parking lot.

0.1 Follow the trail, bearing slightly right (northeast), and reach two rocks large enough to sit on and a trail marker identifying the Oakwell Trail.

0.3 Bear left, heading northwest. Salado Creek is on the right about 20 feet away. There is a path to the creek.

0.6 Continue following the trail northwest through heavy woods. Pass a trail marker on the left stating Tobin Park trailhead is 0.91 miles and the Oakwell trailhead is 0.6 miles.

0.7 Pass a large live oak on the right with branches reaching above and across the trail. Backtrack to the trailhead.

1.4 Arrive back at the trailhead.

14 San Antonio Parks and Recreation: McAllister Park Loop

See white-tailed deer on the fringes of the woodlands while hearing songbirds hidden in the trees. Skirt the edges of baseball diamonds and soccer fields, and strangely enough, at times, you'll seem almost alone in this 986-acre park, San Antonio's largest and most popular. The trail is wheelchair accessible.

Distance: 2.7-mile loop

Approximate hiking time: 1.5 hours

Difficulty: Easy due to flat, wide, paved surface

Trail surface: Asphalt

Best seasons: Year-round

Other trail users: Dog walkers, bikers

Canine compatibility: Leashed dogs permitted

Land status: City park; San Antonio Parks and Recreation Department

Fees and permits: None required

Schedule: 6:00 a.m. to 10:00 p.m. daily

Maps: No maps available at the park. Maps are on the Web site www.sanantonio.gov/sapar/mcallistertrail.asp; USGS Longhorn

Trail contacts: McAllister Park, 13102 Jones–Maltsberger Rd., San Antonio 78247; (210) 207-8480

Finding the trailhead: In San Antonio, from I-410, drive 3.2 miles on US 281 to Bitters Road. Turn east onto Bitters Road and go to the junction with Starcrest. Turn left onto Starcrest and continue to Jones–Maltsberger Road. Turn left onto Jones–Maltsberger and proceed 1 mile to the park entrance on the right, at 13102 Jones–Maltsberger. *DeLorme: Texas Atlas & Gazetteer:* Page 157 F9; page 77 A12. GPS: N 29 32.849' / W 98 27.121'

The Hike

A convenient starting point is on the asphalt trail near Mud Creek and the baseball diamonds. The trail, even though closely bordered by trees, is wide enough to accommodate walkers, joggers, and cyclists. The baseball diamonds and soccer fields on the east side of the park are sometimes visible but go almost unnoticed. There are several well-marked road crossings, so use care. Cross Mud Creek and pass under huge live oaks bordering the trail that create a sense of a pristine area.

The park, created in 1968, was originally called Northeast Preserve. It was renamed in 1974 to honor former San Antonio Mayor Walter W. McAllister. Portions of the park were developed on a floodplain to help protect the San Antonio International Airport. A dam has been built to help control the water level in the Upper Salado Creek watershed. Considering the nearness of the airport, the park has areas that seem pristine, and the woods muffle much of the noise from the air traffic.

Many paths made by overzealous "explorers" crisscross the official 3-mile asphalt trail. Stay on the asphalt trail because some areas in the park are ecologically sensitive. There is no official trailhead, but there are entry spots from numerous parking areas. It is one of the few parks where this capability exists and allows the 3-mile route to be shortened with no worry about getting disoriented.

Huge live oak trees can be seen near drainage waterways in the lower areas. The trees achieved their unusual size because they could not be cut, as they were in a floodplain. They have created a large wooded area that is home to white-tailed deer, rabbits, squirrels, and other wildlife. The

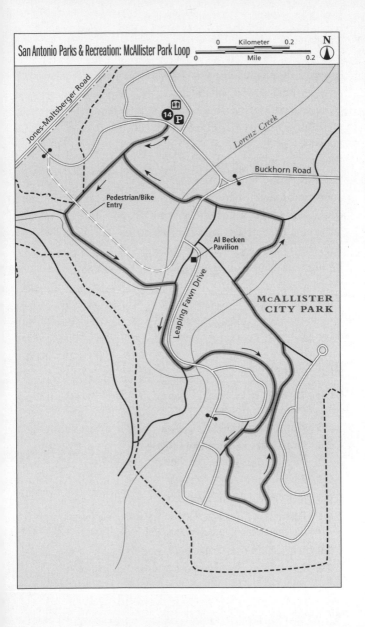

San Antonio Parks & Recreation: McAllister Park Loop

Jones-Maltsberger Road

Lorenz Creek

Buckhorn Road

Pedestrian/Bike Entry

Al Becken Pavilion

Leaping Fawn Drive

McALLISTER CITY PARK

N

0   Kilometer   0.2
0   Mile   0.2

largest concentration of birds, squirrels, and other animals is near the picnic area, where they scavenge the crumbs dropped by picnickers.

The upland area of the park had been used as a dairy farm, and as a result there are a few cedar trees and some mesquite overgrowth. The San Antonio Road Runners and Harmony Hills Optimist Club have helped construct several of the trails in the park.

This park is an anomaly. It's in a major city, on a flood-plain, adjoining a major airport, has baseball diamonds, soccer fields, and a police substation, yet McAllister Park has become a favorite hiking destination for folks living in San Antonio. They appreciate its convenient location, the easy hiking trail that is suitable for all ages, the shaded and sometimes almost secluded areas, and the opportunity to relax while watching white-tailed deer and listening to the many species of birds. It's a great getaway that can be utilized even during a lunch break.

Miles and Directions

NOTE: **The route could change depending on where you enter the trail.**

0.0 Start at the trailhead by the parking lot and head southwest.

0.1 Cross Buckhorn Road and continue southeast until reaching a Y. Take the right branch, heading south.

0.2 Cross the pedestrian entry walk. Continue straight.

0.3 Make a hard left, heading southeast.

0.6 Pass by the Al Becken Pavilion and another trailhead. At the trail intersection, turn right, heading south.

0.8 Turn left, heading southeast. A park road is on the left.

1.0 Turn left, heading east; cross Lorenz Creek and immediately cross Leaping Fawn Drive. Be cautious of automobile traffic.

1.2 Curve right (south). Pass a trail on the right; stay to the left, heading southwest.

1.4 Make a hard left, heading southeast, and then continue straight.

1.5 Take another hard left, this time toward the north-northeast.

1.8 A trail comes in from the right. Continue straight, which is the left branch, heading north-northwest.

2.0 Turn right, heading northeast.

2.2 Turn left (west).

2.4 Pass a trail on the left. Continue straight and then cross Buckhorn Road. Be cautious of automobile traffic.

2.6 Rejoin the original trail at the Y, turning right and retracing your steps toward the trailhead.

2.7 Arrive back at the trailhead.

15 Hill Country State Natural Area: Wilderness and Twin Peaks Trails

Sections of the Wilderness Trail combined with the Twin Peaks Trail is hiking at its best. Go through canyons, up and down rocky hills, and across seasonal creeks to see some of the best scenery in central Texas. The small loop around the Twin Peaks, which are more than 1,800 feet high, has spectacular views. This hike is not recommended for young children.

Distance: 3 miles; interconnecting loops

Approximate hiking time: 2 hours

Difficulty: Easy except for a few steep inclines, which are challenging

Trail surface: Dirt, sand, and loose rock

Best seasons: Sept through June

Other trail users: Equestrians, mountain bikers, dog walkers

Canine compatibility: Leashed dogs permitted

Land status: State natural area; Texas Parks & Wildlife Department

Fees and permits: Fee required, or use the State Parks Pass

Schedule: Dawn to dusk daily

Maps: USGS Tarpley Pass and Twin Hollows quads. Trail maps are also available in the park

office and on the Web site www .tpwd.state.tx.us.

Trail contacts: Hill Country State Natural Area, 10600 Bandera Creek Rd., Bandera 78003; (830) 796-4413; www.tpwd .state.tx.us

Special considerations: Potable water is not available in the park. Bring drinking water. Trails may be subject to closure during wet conditions. Public hunts are held during December and January and the park is closed to the general public. Check the park's calendar for access restrictions. Call the park for specific dates. There is no electricity available in the park. Stay on the designated trails, or receive a citation from a park ranger.

Finding the trailhead: From San Antonio, take TX 16 northwest to Bandera, then take TX 173 south, across the Medina River, to Ranch Road 1077. Turn right and drive 10 miles to where the pavement ends and the road becomes gravel. From here, follow the signs to the park headquarters area. Obtain a permit and then continue on the park road, heading west, to the trailhead parking, which is at the entrance to the camping area (sites #213–#217). The trailhead is about 0.1 mile from the parking area. Hill Country State Natural Area is 40 miles northwest of San Antonio. *DeLorme: Texas Atlas & Gazetteer:* Page 77 A8. GPS: N 29 38.020' / W 99 11.090'

The Hike

Start the Wilderness Trail between campsites #215 and #216 at the trailhead for Trail 1. Keep in mind the warning a ranger gave about this being a primitive area: "We are a primitive park. If you think you need it, we don't got it— you'll need to bring it!" This is in keeping with the stipulation from Louise Merrick of the Merrick Bar-O-Ranch when she donated the land, that it ". . . be kept far removed and untouched by modern civilization, where everything is preserved intact, yet put to useful activities."

The route combines sections of Trail 1 (Wilderness Trail, partial loop), Trail 5 (Twin Peaks), and Trail 5b (west peak of the Twin Peaks lollipop).

Head south on Trail 1 (Wilderness Trail), which is doubletrack and mainly flat. There are four branches with other trails within the first mile, so the hike can be altered to lengthen or decrease the distance. Pass these branches and continue on Wilderness Trail. This is a multiuse trail enjoyed by equestrians, so avoid the manure left by their horses. Look around for dung beetles, unusual in Texas parks, which help clean up the area by feeding on and breeding in the dung.

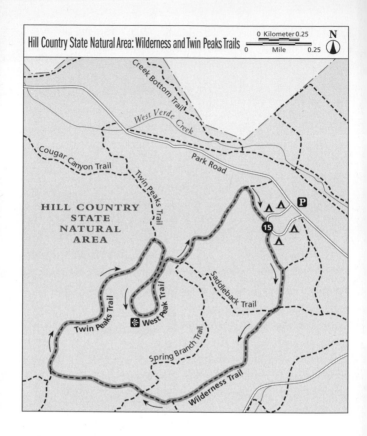

Swing left, bearing west to a gap. There is a park boundary fence; make a hard right going northeast onto Trail 5, the Twin Peaks Trail. Within a short distance, the trail becomes very steep and rugged. This is the most strenuous portion of the hike. A few wild goats enjoy grazing on these hillsides, and jackrabbits take 15-foot hops to escape anything they think is a predator. Western diamondback rattlesnakes call the Hill Country home and may be seen while hiking. Learn to recognize the venomous snakes (rattlesnakes and water moccasins) from the nonvenomous, so everything that slithers doesn't unnerve you.

Continue heading northeast until Trail 5 branches left and the short Trail 5b loop goes right. Take the loop heading up to the West Peak. This trail is rocky and challenging. Enjoy the 360-degree panorama from 1,870 feet up, as the loop circles the top. This is one of the best spots to appreciate the park's 5,400 acres. The loop ends and leads to markers for Trail 5, which heads downhill toward the campsites. Patches of sotol, a plant resembling yucca but with less-rigid leaves, hang over many trails.

This is one of the best hikes in the entire Hill Country region because it explores many of the different environments the Hill Country offers, while offering a rigorous, scenic walk.

Miles and Directions

0.0 Start at the Wilderness Trail (Trail 1) trailhead. (It's about 0.1 mile from the parking area.)

0.3 Singletrack Trail 5a crosses Trail 1. Continue straight on Trail 1.

0.8 Trail 1a intersects on the left (south) and dead-ends at Trail 1. Continue forward, veering right.

0.9 Singletrack Trail 6 crosses Trail 1. Continue on Trail 1.

1.3 The trail branches near a gap at the fence. Turn right (north) onto singletrack Trail 5. Prepare for a very steep climb. The trail has loose rocks scattered on it, making walking precarious.

2.0 Finish the climb and come to a branch. Turn right onto Trail 5a, heading southeast.

2.1 Trail 5b intersects Trail 5a. Turn right and continue on Trail 5b. This steep climb takes you up to Twin Peaks. Follow the loop to the left on Trail 5b. There's an observation point with panoramic views. Complete the loop and then backtrack to the intersection with Trail 5a.

2.4 Trail 5b T branches into Trail 5a. Turn right, heading east.

2.5 Come to a T branch with Trail 6. Turn left onto Trail 6, heading northeast, and begin the easy downhill walk to campsites 214 and 215.

3.0 Arrive back at the trailhead.

16 Cibolo Nature Center: Prairie, Creekside, and Woodlands Trails

Along the Creekside Trail, towering bald cypress trees create a canopy for singing birds and darting dragonflies. Look into the clear water of Cibolo Creek to see red-eared slider turtles and catfish. After the hike, look at the castings of the dinosaur tracks near the pavilion. This hike will even hold the interest of young hikers.

Distance: 2.2 miles; interconnecting loops

Approximate hiking time: 1.5 hours

Difficulty: Easy except for the short uphill path that connects to Woodlands Trail

Trail surface: Forested dirt path

Best seasons: Year-round

Other trail users: Equestrians, dog walkers

Canine compatibility: Leashed dogs permitted

Land status: City park; City of Boerne

Fees and permits: None required

Schedule: Trails open 8:00 a.m. to dark daily; park open Monday through Friday 9:00 a.m. to 5:00 p.m.; Saturday 9:00 a.m. to 1:00 p.m.

Maps: A map is included in a brochure, available in the visitor center; USGS Boerne

Trail contacts: Cibolo Nature Center, 140 City Park Rd./P.O. Box 9, Boerne 78006; (830) 249-4616; www.cibolo.org

Finding the trailhead: From San Antonio, take I-10 north about 30 miles to the first Boerne exit, exit 542, which is for TX 87 northbound. Follow TX 87 north through the intersection with TX 46 westbound. Turn right onto River Road (TX 46 east), which parallels Cibolo Creek. Continue on TX 46 eastbound for about 1 mile and turn right onto City Park Road. Take City Park Road almost to its end and turn right into the Cibolo Nature Center. Cibolo Nature Center is

30 miles northwest of San Antonio. *DeLorme: Texas Atlas & Gazetteer:* Page 68 J5. GPS: N 29 46.508' / W 98 42.817'

The Hike

Start at the trailhead located north of the visitor center. There is a pavilion and building close to the trailhead that has restrooms and a large mural-type map of the park painted on the wall. Go down a few steps and almost immediately cross a bridge, then head south onto the Woodlands Trail. There is a reclaimed pocket prairie to the right containing big bluestem grass, switchgrass, and Indian grass. This is the type of grass seen in western prairie paintings from the 1900s, where the grass was taller than the belly of a horse.

The trail stays close to the creek, and several paths lead down to the edge. Large bald cypresses, along with some dogwood and basswood trees, line the shoreline. Red-eared slider turtles sunning themselves congregate on logs protruding from the water.

Pass a stone stairway on the right (west) leading up to the Creekside Trail. The creek widens a bit here, and there are large boulders that must be navigated around. The creek is nearby on the right, and a bluff is bordering the left.

One of the best ways to identify and learn about what animals have been near the trail is to look for signs such as tracks. The tracks of raccoons, skunks, armadillos, and deer are easy to identify and can usually be found near the creek. This type of "search and identify" activity can even be enjoyed by very young hikers.

At the next stairway turn right, heading west away from the creek and up the stairs. They are made from stone and are very steep. The stairway acts as the connector to the Creekside Trail.

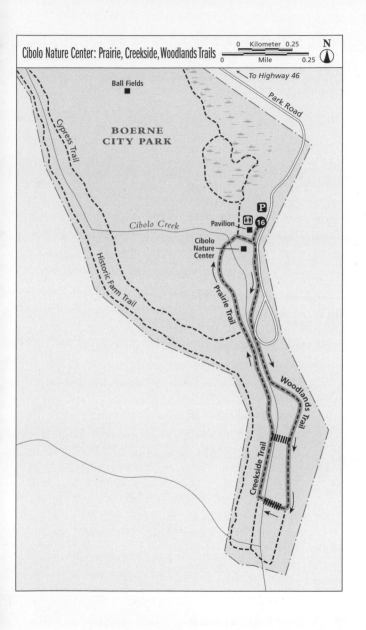

Cibolo Nature Center: Prairie, Creekside, Woodlands Trails

Ball Fields

BOERNE
CITY PARK

Cypress Trail

Cibolo Creek

Historic Farm Trail

To Highway 46

Park Road

Pavilion

Cibolo Nature Center

Prairie Trail

Woodlands Trail

Creekside Trail

The scenery abruptly changes at the top of the hill, from the riparian forest that's along the creek to the live oak savanna on top of the bluff. Ecologists call this transition zone between two different plant communities an ecotone.

Follow the trail on top of the bluff as it heads away from the creek. The trees scattered along the trail are mostly cedar, and prickly pear cactus is abundant. The trail then runs parallel with an electrified wire fence that marks the park boundary. Pass a small picnic area and then continue following the trail to the visitor center.

Be sure to check out the 80-foot-long set of castings of dinosaur tracks near the pavilion. It is believed the larger tracks were made by an *Acrocanthosaurus*, a 40-foot-long, three-ton, meat-eating dinosaur that walked on its two hind legs.

Miles and Directions

- **0.0** Start at the Prairie Trail trailhead, which is located north of the visitor center.
- **0.1** The trail branches to a shelter and picnic table. Take the left branch, heading south.
- **0.6** Cross a small seasonal stream leading to the creek.
- **0.7** Pass a set of steps on the right that connect to the Creekside Trail. Continue south on the Woodlands Trail.
- **0.8** A very steep stone stairway acts as another connector to the Creekside Trail. At the top of the stairs, turn right onto Creekside Trail, going north. Cibolo Creek will be on your right.
- **0.9** The Cypress Trail intersects on the left (west) and ends at the Creekside Trail. Continue straight (north). The Creekside Trail becomes the Prairie Trail.

1.5 Follow the Prairie Trail north. Continue north and bear slighty right.

2.2 Arrive back at the trailhead.

17 Medina River Park: El Camino and Rio Medina Trails

This is a nature and river lovers' park. Start on the El Camino Trail, a concrete, wheelchair–accessible path that goes to an overlook on the Medina River. Pick up the Rio Medina Trail and follow the river through the natural area. The riparian area features large cottonwoods, native pecans, and bald cypress trees. All the ingredients for a natural area are here, including a river, wild hogs, maybe a snake, poison ivy, wildflowers, and many colorful birds, lizards, and butterflies. The park is a great place to kick back and enjoy.

Distance: 3-mile lollipop loop
Approximate hiking time: 1.75 hours
Difficulty: Easy due to small paved section
Trail surface: Concrete; dirt path
Best seasons: Sept through June
Other trail users: Joggers
Canine compatibility: Dogs not permitted
Land status: San Antonio natural area park; San Antonio Parks and Recreation Department

Fees and permits: No fees or permits required
Schedule: 7:30 a.m. to sundown daily; closed Christmas and New Year's Day
Maps: A trail map is available in the park office. A map may be printed from www.sanantonio.gov/sapar/pdf/medinatrailmap.pdf
Trail contacts: Medina River Park, 15890 Highway 16 South, San Antonio 78264; (210) 624-2575; www.sanantonio.gov/sapar

Finding the trailhead: From San Antonio's I-410, drive 4.2 miles south on TX 16. The park entrance is on the left (east) side just before the Medina River bridge. The trailhead is at the start of a wide, wheelchair-accessible concrete walk, about 90 yards west

of the park office. Start at the park office, pick up a map, and head
west to the trailhead. *DeLorme: Texas Atlas & Gazetteer:* Page 77
D11. GPS: N 29 15.300' / W 98 34.421'

The Hike

Medina River Park is the city's first natural area park in
south Bexar County. In spring brightly colored birds,
including painted buntings, indigo buntings, and cedar
waxwings, may be observed in the wildflower area near the
office.

From the trailhead, follow the twisting and turning El
Camino Trail. A low stone fence is on the left where the
trail makes a gradual bend going right. Pass a large open-
sided pavilion that has picnic tables, grills, and a water
fountain. The Medina River is on the right. The El Camino
Trail ends at a cleared area that overlooks the river. Benches
are placed at intervals along the trail.

The trail branches right (south) to the gravel-surfaced
Rio Medina Trail. Poison ivy, some bushy and some climbing up trees, is on both the right and left. Underbrush and
pecan trees, the state tree, are on a hill to the left. The bald
cypress trees lining the riverbank are unusual in that they
have no exposed "knees" jutting up from the water. The
rangers have no explanation for this.

Farther on, a steep footpath goes about 125 feet down to
the river, giving hikers an opportunity to explore the river's
edge. Pecan trees at the trail's edge keep getting larger,
while cottonwoods and hackberries line the river's edge.
Keep going straight on the Rio Medina Trail, which turns
to dirt, with the forest and undergrowth getting denser.

There is a shallow gully on the right. Wild mustang
grapevines are abundant, and many Texans make jelly from

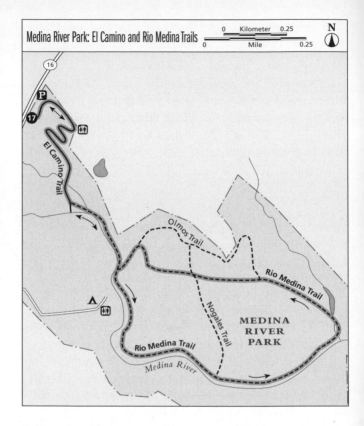

the grapes; these are very bitter and acidic, not to be eaten raw. In the spring, wildflowers such as gaillardia, winecup, and verbena are in bloom, inviting numerous butterflies, including gulf fritillaries and swallowtails, to gather their nectar. Watch for green kingfishers sitting in tree branches along the river, waiting for an opportunity to have a fish dinner. Follow the trail left and head up a steep grade.

As the trail continues to bear left, heading west, the river makes a right turn, going east, and disappears. The Rio

Medina Trail, which is wide and grassy at this point, continues straight (west). Wild hogs are prevalent; watch for tracks and places where the ground has been rooted up.

Come to a T; the right leg is the Olmos Trail. Stay left and shortly reach the interpretive path that was passed early in the hike. Bear right (north) at this juncture, retrace the Rio Medina Trail to where it joins the concrete El Camino Trail, and return to the trailhead.

Miles and Directions

0.0 Start at the El Camino trailhead about 90 yards west of the park office at Medina River Park.

0.4 Reach the Medina River Overlook and the branch with the Rio Medina Trail. Take the right (south) leg onto the Rio Medina Trail, which has a gravel surface.

1.1 The connector Nogales Trail intersects and ends on the left (north) side of the Rio Medina Trail. Continue heading east on Rio Medina.

1.6 The Olmos Trail intersects and ends on the right (north) side of Rio Medina. Continue heading west on Rio Medina.

2.0 The section of the Rio Medina Trail with the natural surface meets the graveled section near the path to the river and the interpretive area. Turn right (north) and retrace the path taken at the beginning of the hike.

2.6 The Rio Medina Trail joins the concrete El Camino Trail at the Medina River Overlook. Continue straight onto the El Camino Trail and backtrack to the trailhead.

3.0 Arrive back at the trailhead.

18 Palmetto State Park: Hiking Trail

Nature lovers will enjoy the trail as it passes near the San Marcos River. The area contains perfect habitat for birds, frogs, insects, and possibly a snake or two. Watch for springs in the swampy area, which many years ago contained hot springs and mud boils.

Distance: 2.4-mile lollipop
Approximate hiking time: 1 hour
Difficulty: Easy, mostly flat, shaded trail
Trail surface: Dirt
Best seasons: Year-round
Other trail users: Dog walkers
Canine compatibility: Leashed dogs permitted
Land status: State park; Texas Parks & Wildlife Department
Fees and permits: Fee required, or use the State Parks Pass
Schedule: 8:00 a.m. to 10:00 p.m. daily

Maps: Trail maps are available in the park office. You can also find maps on the Web site www.tpwd .state.tx.us; USGS Ottine
Trail contacts: Palmetto State Park, Park Road, 11 South, Gonzales 78629; (830) 672-3266; www.tpwd.state.us
Special considerations: The trail is not well marked, and many paths have been made by campers. Water moccasins and rattlesnakes, both venomous, are in the park but are seldom seen and rarely encountered.

Finding the trailhead: To reach the park from Gonzales, travel 10 miles northwest on US 183 to FM 1586. Go west on FM 1586 for 2 miles to Ottine, then south on PR 11 for 2 miles to park headquarters. *DeLorme: Texas Atlas & Gazetteer:* Page 78 A5. GPS: N 29 35.367' / W 97 34.920'

The Hike

See the remnants of hot springs, which, in the 1930s, people thought cured polio. From the trailhead, pass a small clearing where a few dwarf palmettos are growing beneath taller trees. The woods continue for the balance of the hike and furnish welcome shade.

After completing a couple of turns, come to a sign on the left that indicates the presence of a mud boil. Look hard—there is no boiling mud, just a wet depression in the ground near the sign. Prior to the 1970s, this area was wetter and had more thermal activity, including hot springs that created mud boils. This activity probably ended due to changes brought about by the widespread drilling for oil and water.

At the turn of the century, the swamp was a major attraction to visitors seeking the healing powers of the hot springs. The Warm Springs Foundation in Ottine was established in 1937, to use the waters in the treatment of polio. Many artesian wells and flowing springs can still be found in the park today.

The trail squiggles around and the terrain remains flat. Head east past the south side of the modern camping area and skirt campsites #9 to #19. Heavy woods and undergrowth keep the campground from view. Although raccoons are normally nocturnal animals, a few "beggars" may be seen gathering food near the campground. The palmettos have all but disappeared here; they've been replaced by oak, elm, and hackberry trees. Stray paths intercept the trail. Pass a gully on the right and continue right as another stray path branches off.

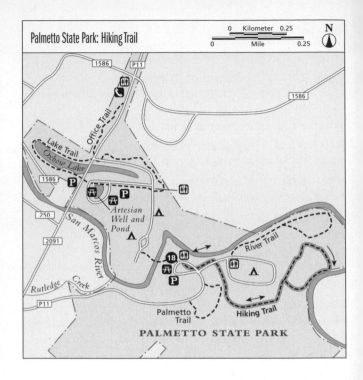

The trail veers to the right and heads into a marshy area near the San Marcos River. This is an area alive with sound, including the hum of insects, the beeping of frogs, and the calls of numerous birds being heard but not seen.

At the next branch take the right leg, which leads to a short but steep grade. This is the first minor change in elevation. The campground is on the right, and several paths lead to campsite #9. At the top of the incline, continue straight and backtrack to the trailhead.

Miles and Directions

0.0 Start at the Hiking Trail trailhead.

0.9 Reach the junction where the Hiking Trail loop connects to itself. Continue straight. Follow the loop around, bearing right.

1.5 Return to the junction where the Hiking Trail loop connects. Backtrack toward the trailhead.

2.4 Arrive back at the trailhead.

19 Palmetto State Park: Palmetto and Lake Trails

Palmetto State Park offers excellent short trail options that can be hiked during a single outing. Palmetto Trail and Lake Trail have been combined into a single hike. The Palmetto Trail conjures scenes from the film *Jurassic Park*, with clinging vines, dwarf palmettos, and green ponds in the Ottine Swamp. Lake Trail circles the four-acre Oxbow Lake, formed by the meandering San Marcos River, which offers a variety of vegetation and possibly some water snakes.

Distance: 1 mile for both (0.3-mile Palmetto Trail, lollipop; 0.7-mile Lake Trail, loop)

Approximate hiking time: 0.75 hour total

Difficulty: Easy due to the level terrain and good shade

Trail surface: Dirt

Best seasons: Year-round

Other trail users: Dog walkers

Canine compatibility: Leashed dogs permitted

Land status: State park; Texas Parks & Wildlife Department

Fees and permits: Fee required, or use the State Parks Pass

Schedule: 8:00 a.m. to 10:00 p.m. daily

Maps: Trail maps are available in the park office. You can also find maps on the Web site www.tpwd.state.tx.us; USGS Ottine

Trail contacts: Palmetto State Park, Park Road 11 South, Gonzales 78629; (830) 672-3266

Finding the trailhead: To reach the park from Gonzales, travel 10 miles northwest on US 183 to FM 1586. Go west on FM 1586 for 2 miles to Ottine, then south on PR 11 for 2 miles to park headquarters. *DeLorme: Texas Atlas & Gazetteer:* Page 78 A5. GPS: N 29 35.367' / W 97 34.920'

The Hike

Palmetto Trail

The Palmetto Trail is a self-guided walk with numbered markers, which are referenced in an interpretive guide available near the trailhead. This flat, well-marked trail is wheelchair accessible. The shift in elevation is nominal, but the shift in vegetation is remarkable. This short walk is the signature hike of the park.

Pass several plant identification markers and then cross a footbridge over a swampy area. A sign on the left tells about the hydraulic ram-jet pump located there, one of the few operational ram-jet pumps in existence. This pump uses no electricity—instead, the energy of water flowing from an artesian well moves the water from below ground to the water storage tower.

Thick stands of dwarf palmettos, only 3 to 4 feet tall, are on both sides of the trail. These palms, spaced between ephemeral lagoons in the Ottine Swamp, cause thoughts of *Jurassic Park*.

Pass a gully on the right, go by a large sycamore tree dressed with a trumpet vine with bright orange flowers, and then cross a footbridge over a narrow, dry creek bed. Burr oak trees line the trail and are easily identified in the fall by the large acorns with a fringe around the cap that are scattered on the ground.

The loop ends back at PR 11; from there take PR 11 to the Lake Trail trailhead next to campsite 26.

NOTE: There are no Miles and Directions provided for this short 0.3-mile hike.

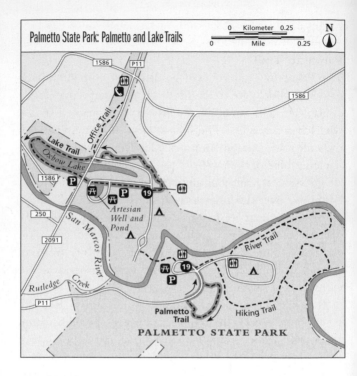

Palmetto State Park: Palmetto and Lake Trails

1586 P11

1586

Office Trail

Lake Trail

Oxbow Lake

1586 P 19

250 Artesian Well and Pond

2091 San Marcos River

River Trail

19 P

Rutledge Creek

P11

Palmetto Trail

Hiking Trail

PALMETTO STATE PARK

0 Kilometer 0.25
0 Mile 0.25

N

Lake Trail

Lake Trail is a short walk that circles Oxbow Lake. In the spring, damselflies, dragonflies, butterflies, and mosquitoes are abundant from ground level to head height.

From the trailhead, head into a swampy, wooded area, then slightly downhill and left to a wooden bridge. Oxbow Lake can be seen to the left. The four-acre lake was created when the slow-moving San Marcos River changed directions and left an isolated lagoon. Turn left where the trail branches; the right leg leads to the park office.

The trail wanders away from the lake and then heads back to a long clearing that extends to the water's edge.

This gives an opportunity to observe various water insects, including water striders. A good view of the entire lake can be seen from here.

Make a bend left and head south, continuing on the loop around the lake. The Little Hill Baptist Church is ahead and to the right. Continue straight and cross under the PR 11 bridge that spans the lake. On the other side of the bridge, there is a large sign warning about snakes.

The trail ends near the bridge, but continue east, skirting the edge of a picnic area and past campground sites #20 to #24, to the parking lot.

Miles and Directions

0.0 Start at the Lake Trail trailhead, located to the left and behind the restrooms next to campsite #26.

0.2 Cross PR 11 at the bridge. Continue following the loop along the lake, going generally west and then curving around the end of the lake to head east.

0.3 Cross PR 11 at the bridge. Continue past the play field and campsites, heading for the parking lot.

0.7 Arrive back at the trailhead.

About the Author

Keith Stelter is a columnist for the HCN newspaper group and has been hiking, writing, and taking photographs for forty years. Keith served as executive director of the Texas Outdoor Writers Association during 2006 and 2007. His other FalconGuides include *Best Hikes Near Austin and San Antonio* and Best Easy Day Hikes guides to Houston and Austin. He is a member of the Outdoor Writers Association of America, Texas Master Naturalists, North American Nature Photographers Association, and American Trails Association. He currently resides in Tomball, Texas.